THE ABUNDANT WALLET

Smart Methods for Mastering Money

LARRY TUCH

FOREWORD BY : CALEB GUILLIAMS
FOUNDER - BETTERWEALTH.COM

Larry Tuch-- 1st ed.
Chief Editor, Shannon Buritz
ISBN: 978-1-954757-56-1

The Publisher has strived to be as accurate and complete as possible in the creation of this book.

This book is not intended for use as a legal, business, accounting, or financial advice source. All readers are advised to seek the services of competent professionals in legal, business, accounting, and finance fields.

Like anything else in life, there are no guarantees of income or results in practical advice books. Readers are cautioned to rely on their judgment about their individual circumstances to act accordingly.

While all attempts have been made to verify information provided in this publication, the Publisher assumes no responsibility for errors, omissions, or contrary interpretation of the subject matter herein. Any perceived slights of specific persons, peoples, or organizations are unintentional.

To Arlene, your unwavering support, encouragement, and love have carried me through every page of this journey. Thanks for believing in me even when I doubted myself.

To my incredible children, Maddie and Sam, you inspire me to dream bigger and reach higher every day. This book is as much for you as it is for me.

To my friends and family, thank you for your encouragement, patience, and belief in my vision. Your support has meant everything.

To my publisher and editor, your guidance and partnership made this dream a reality, and I'm deeply grateful.

And to you, the reader, thank you for taking the time to walk through this journey with me. Your belief in these words means more than you know. From the bottom of my heart - thank you.

CONTENTS

FOREWORD

When I first met Larry, I was immediately struck by his humility, his hunger, and his heart. This is someone who didn't come from money. He spent nearly two decades living paycheck to paycheck and dealing with bad debt. And yet, he had the courage not only to turn his life around but also to write about it, not just for himself in a journal, but to share his story so that others could be inspired by it.

Larry is a perfect example of someone whose past didn't dictate his future. He faced imposter syndrome head-on, leaned into masterminds, began investing in real estate, lived on less than half of his income, discovered the power of cash value life insurance, and—step by step—built what he now calls *The Abundant Wallet Method*. It's a powerful, intentional way to build wealth. And what's more, he doesn't just use it for himself; he helps others do the same.

In his book, Larry covers many powerful ideas, but four themes especially stood out to me:

- **Challenging the Status Quo** – It's easy to accept, "This is how it's always been done," but Larry challenges that thinking. He questions whether plans like the traditional 401(k)s are right for everyone and invites readers to explore alternatives based on their unique goals.

- **Mindset as Your Foundation** – Larry emphasizes how critical it is to move beyond a scarcity mindset and begin to see yourself as your greatest asset. That shift in thinking can transform everything.

- **Real Estate as a Wealth Tool** – While many overcomplicate it, Larry simplifies the path. When structured correctly, real estate can appreciate, generate cash flow, offer tax advantages, and create leverage. Larry breaks it down in a way that's both approachable and powerful, showing how financial freedom — having enough passive income to cover your expenses —can become possible through real estate. He also shares practical ways to learn more and take the next steps.

- **The Power of Life Insurance** – Perhaps one of the most misunderstood asset classes, life insurance is often misused or dismissed. Larry teaches how, when used correctly, it can give your dollars multiple jobs, protect your family, and serve as a financial foundation that empowers everything else.

Overall, I want to congratulate Larry on writing this book. I'm excited about the lives it will impact, and I was personally encouraged by the reminders it gave me about how to live more intentionally.

At BetterWealth, our vision is to make intentional living the new wealth standard because if you're not living intentionally, you're not truly wealthy. Larry, you and this book are a great example of what it looks like to take ownership of your past, inspire others toward a more intentional future, and offer a blueprint for how to get there.

As you read this book, remember that you have only one life. You may have already lived a good chunk of it; please give yourself permission to live it intentionally and to the fullness.

Caleb Guilliams
Founder - BetterWealth.com

INTRODUCTION

Imagine a life where you have enough money in the bank to live on your own terms. Whether it's retiring early, launching a new business venture, or funding your children's education, the common thread is control—over your money, your future, and your freedom. In this book, I want to show you how to take that control, become your own bank, and create an abundant life where your money works for you behind the scenes, creating opportunities without extra effort on your part.

If you're like many people, the idea of being financially self-sufficient might seem too good to be true. You've probably heard advice from well-known financial personalities, and maybe they've told you that strategies like the one I will share with you in this book aren't realistic. When something sounds different from the advice we've grown up hearing, it's easy to dismiss it. "This must be a scam," some people think. Others believe significant risk must be involved to make excellent returns or assume that strategies like this are only available to the wealthy, not the working class. But I can assure you, *The Abundant Wallet* method is not just for the rich or some elite group. It's for anyone who is ready to take control of their money and let it work for them.

One of the biggest barriers to financial self-sufficiency is the traditional advice ingrained in society. People are told to rely on government plans like 401(k)s and IRAs for retirement, but here's the catch: you don't actually own those plans—the government does. They set the rules and dictate how much you can contribute, when you can withdraw, and how much they'll tax you. These limitations create a false sense of security and restrict your ability to grow wealth on your terms.

If you follow the herd, you're following a system designed to maintain the status quo. The media, financial personalities, and traditional retirement plans encourage a mindset that works for the middle class—not for those striving to achieve greater financial independence.

Think about it: people like Dave Ramsey and Suze Orman focus on debt as the enemy. While that advice works for some, it overlooks the fact that not all debt is bad. Good debt—debt that funds income-producing assets—can help you build wealth passively or semi-passively. The key is knowing how to use debt to your advantage.

Fear often stands in the way of becoming financially self-sufficient. For those with an investor mindset, the biggest concern might be whether *The Abundant Wallet* strategy can quickly generate enough money to fund their next big venture. Others might worry about liquidity—whether they can access their money when they need it.

There's also a tendency to compare different approaches to traditional retirement methods, leading to fears about safety and potential returns. Concerns about taxes often come into play as well. People worry that they'll lose out due to tax implications or that this method isn't secure enough to protect their money.

These fears are valid but rooted in a misunderstanding of how this strategy works. Let me assure you: this method doesn't involve taking wild risks or locking your money away. The tools I'll share are flexible and designed to work for every income level.

In the following pages, we'll explore the answers to some of the most common questions my clients have about *The Abundant Wallet* method, including:

- *"How much do I have to invest?"*
- *"What happens if I have an illness?"*
- *"What type of documentation, proof of income, paystubs, or debt do I need to get started?*
- *"Why haven't I heard of this before?"*

I created *The Abundant Wallet* because I've been where you are. Five years ago, I was stuck in a storm—living paycheck to paycheck, caught in a cycle that I couldn't escape. For 18 years, I followed the same routines, hoping for different results, until I realized something had to change. They say the definition of insanity is doing the same thing over and over and expecting a different outcome, and I was living proof of that.

So, I made a pivot. I shifted my mindset and decided to try something different. That decision changed everything. Over the past five years, I've dedicated myself to studying and mastering strategies for financial self-sufficiency. I've earned designations and licenses in life, health, and annuities insurance and worked with clients in Florida and several other states. But beyond the credentials, I've lived this process. I know what it's like to feel stuck and unsure of the next step. Many of my clients and prospects are where I was just a few years ago, looking for a way out of the financial grind.

I'm not perfect, and I'll never pretend to know everything. But I'm a lifelong learner, always working to improve and expand my knowledge. And if there's ever a situation where I'm not the right person to help you, I'll ensure you're connected with someone who can. That's how committed I am to seeing you succeed.

Some people think of success in terms of how big their pile of money is. But it's really what that money allows you to do and who you become. When you shift from a scarcity mindset to one of abundance, you realize there's enough for everyone. You no longer feel like you're competing with others for limited resources. Instead, you embrace the freedom to build the life you want without limitations.

This abundance mindset doesn't happen overnight. It requires a pivot, a willingness to change how you think about money and success. But once you make that shift, the possibilities are endless. Imagine never having to take out a loan for a car again because you've built your own financial system that works for you. Imagine living below your means, not because you have to, but because you choose to—knowing you can easily make big purchases when they truly matter to you.

We're seeing it everywhere: people leaving corporate jobs in pursuit of freedom and fulfillment. What was once considered a pipe dream is now becoming a reality for many. But here's the truth—those who succeed in this new wave of independence didn't get there without challenges. They made mistakes, pivoted, and found better solutions along the way.

If you are an entrepreneur, you know this journey well. You want the ability to make decisions that align with your goals and values. You want to wake up daily knowing you're not just working for a paycheck but building a life of purpose and opportunity.

This book is my way of sharing everything I've learned, so you don't have to spend years figuring it out on your own. I've lived through the grind of paycheck-to-paycheck living, feeling like there was no way out. But I also discovered that there's a smarter, better way to break free from the limitations we're taught to accept.

Too many people are trapped in a scarcity mindset, a way of thinking passed down through generations. Growing up, I saw it firsthand—my parents, shaped by their parents' experiences during the Great Depression, taught me to be cautious, even fearful, about money. Those lessons, while well-intentioned, created habits and beliefs that kept me stuck. Remember that scarcity isn't a rule—it's a mindset. Mindsets can change.

If you believe there's more to life than just getting by, this book is for you. I want to inspire you to stop comparing yourself to others and focus on your growth. Look back at what you accomplished last year and ask yourself, "How can I do better this year?" If you're ambitious, tired of just letting life happen to you, and ready to take responsibility for your own success, I'm here to guide you. The journey to your abundant wallet starts now.

- Larry Tuch

PART ONE

BUILD THE ABUNDANCE FOUNDATION

CHAPTER ONE

GET INTO THE ABUNDANCE MINDSET

I started out with a scarcity mindset, so I know first-hand how much it can get in your way. You're stuck in a loop of doubt, constantly second-guessing what's possible. A scarcity mindset is like putting blinders on. It keeps you focused on what you *don't* have, what you *can't* do, and what *might* go wrong. You end up blocking yourself from opportunities without even realizing it. And the truth is, shifting out of that mindset doesn't happen overnight. It's a progression. But once your mind is open to abundance, there's nothing you can't do—whether it's as an entrepreneur, an investor, or anything else you set your mind to.

One of my biggest game-changers was *The Secret*, a documentary featuring Bob Proctor and the Law of Attraction. The idea that you can manifest what you want in life, that what you focus on expands, and that you have control over your financial future was eye-opening.

When I was trying to get out of debt, every dollar that left my bank account felt like a loss, an expense, something I would never get back. That kind of thinking makes you hold on too tight, afraid to take risks and invest in yourself. However, I started seeing things differently once I shifted into an abundance mindset.

Now, I look at money as an investment in my business, education, or even lessons I learn when something *doesn't* work out. Sure, on a financial statement, it may look like an expense. But in reality, I'm investing in my future. Even if something didn't go as planned, that money wasn't wasted. I paid for experience. And if that experience saved me from making an even bigger mistake down the road, then it would have been worth every penny.

A scarcity mindset isn't something we're born with. It comes from how we were raised, the beliefs passed down from our families, and the habits we pick up along the way. I grew up thinking that money was *always* scarce and there was never enough to go around.

We live in a world full of opportunity. With the technology and resources we have today, there is more than enough to go around. But you have to be open to seeing it. You have to stop believing the false story that you're not smart enough, not talented enough, or that success is only for a select few.

I've always believed that success is 80% mindset and 20%

skill set. Skills? You can learn them. Nothing is stopping you from picking up what you need along the way. But if your mindset is stuck in scarcity—if you're telling yourself, *"I don't know enough, I'm not ready, I'm not as good as them"*—then you're going to limit your potential. You change your mindset, and you change your future.

How I Learned to Stop Comparing My Level 1 to Someone Else's Level 10

When I got into real estate investing, I had huge imposter syndrome. I had nothing to measure myself against, no baseline to say whether I was doing well or failing miserably. It took me seven months to close my first deal. I don't know if that's fast or slow compared to other people, but in my head, it felt like forever.

During that time, I made the mistake of comparing myself to others. I'd see people closing deals faster and making money quicker, and I let that get in my head. I felt like I was behind. But here's what I realized: **I can't compare my level 1 to someone else's level 10.**

Everyone starts at a different place. Some people have more money, more connections, or just a different set of experiences. And we all learn at our own pace. Instead of measuring myself against others, I started measuring myself against where I started. And that changed everything.

After that first deal—after what felt like an eternity—the following deals came super fast. It was like breaking through a wall. Everything started to click once I got the reps in and built that muscle memory. When you push through the slow start, you hit a point where it becomes second nature.

So, if you're in that phase where things feel slow, where you doubt yourself, where you're watching others succeed and wondering if you're even cut out for this, trust the process. You're building a foundation. And once you break through, everything accelerates.

Questioning the Herd Mentality

One of the biggest mindset shifts I had to make was learning to question the popular path. Most people follow the herd because it feels safe. But I started asking: *"What are the 1% or 2% of highly successful people doing differently? What choices are they making that everyone else isn't?"* Instead of just accepting what "everyone else" is doing, I analyzed data, patterns, and real-life outcomes. And I realized that abundance isn't about luck—it's about perspective.

For a long time, I followed the herd. I believed in the traditional financial advice that gets passed around: put money into a 401(k), max out an IRA, and trust that the stock market will do the rest. And yes, over time, a 401(k) gains about 10% year over year if you ride out the market fluctuations. It's the "safe" way to build wealth, or so I thought.

Then I joined a real estate mastermind group. It was full of entrepreneurs who thought differently. They weren't limited by conventional wisdom. They didn't take anything off the table.

One of them asked me, *"Why don't you tap into your 401(k) for capital?"*

At first, I resisted. Everything I had been taught screamed, *"You're not supposed to do that!"* But then I did my research, and what I found shocked me. Most people don't realize that the 401(k) was never meant to be a retirement plan. It was initially designed to supplement pensions, not replace them. But over time, it became the default retirement vehicle for the masses.

The more I looked into it, the more I saw the limitations. You're capped at $20,000–$25,000 per year, and even if you max it out, your returns are slow and steady but not game-changing. I saw someone proudly post that they had put $65,000 into their Roth IRA over ten years and had gained $35,000 in compounded interest. To me, that was too safe.

Meanwhile, I was looking at real estate deals where flipping a property could bring in $15,000 to $20,000 in six months or $40,000 to $50,000 in two to three years. That's when I realized there are smarter, faster ways to grow wealth if you're willing to think outside the box.

I don't believe high returns are just for "certain people" or the ultra-wealthy. Anyone can do this. The difference is that some people do the research and take action, while others stick to traditional, slow-burn methods.

For me, it's about efficiency. If there's a way to make more money in less time, I want to learn it. If a strategy challenges the status quo but produces results, I'm all in. I don't just follow the popular path—I analyze the smartest vehicles for building wealth and then take action.

Learning About Money the Hard Way

Growing up, money was a taboo subject in my family. My parents had a very traditional mindset. They believed in going to college, studying hard, getting a good-paying job, and sticking with it. That was their version of financial security. And looking back, I get it. For them, working for someone else, collecting a steady paycheck, and getting benefits felt safe. And in many ways, it was. But I didn't realize then that safety can also be a trap that keeps you from seeing bigger opportunities.

There were no financial mentors in my life growing up. No one taught me about investing, building wealth, or thinking beyond a paycheck. I had to figure it all out on my own. And back then—before the internet—you couldn't just Google "how to build wealth" or find a financial coach with a quick search. If there were professionals out there sharing financial knowledge in the '80s and '90s, I sure didn't know where to find them.

Without financial literacy, you don't even know what you *don't* know. That was my reality. I followed traditional strategies because that was all I had been exposed to. It wasn't until my late 20s and early 30s that I started to question whether there was another way. That's when I first discovered the idea of financial coaching. There were people who actually studied money, investments, and strategies for building wealth.

If you don't educate yourself financially, you'll always be stuck in someone else's system. Whether that's a job, a retirement plan, or just a limited mindset about what's possible, you can't break free if you don't know what's out there. The first thing I did was immerse myself in education. I started reading financial books, watching YouTube videos, and diving into success stories of people who had built wealth on their own terms. I wanted to understand how money really worked, not just how society told me to manage it.

Once I had the knowledge, I joined a real estate mastermind group for two years and a financial coaching mastermind group for six months. For the first time, I was surrounded by mentors who wanted to help. They were willing to share their thought process, break things down step by step, and guide me through the journey. That level of support was something I had never experienced before, and it gave me the confidence to take real action.

Becoming My Own Bank

The idea that I could take complete control of my financial future, that I didn't have to rely on government-backed retirement plans, and that I could become my own bank completely changed my perspective. It all comes down to income-producing assets. That's the key. When you start focusing on assets that generate wealth instead of just saving money and hoping for the best, you break free from the scarcity mindset and step into abundance.

When I first started shifting into an abundance mindset, I had no idea how much of an impact it would have on the people around me. At the time, I wasn't actively trying to change lives or bring people into real estate investing; I was just documenting my journey. I'd post on my Facebook story whenever I put in an offer on a house, closed a deal, or took a new step in my financial journey. I wasn't pitching anything or trying to convince anyone to invest; I was just sharing.

At first, most people didn't get it. I'd post about a property I was investing in, and someone would ask, *"Wait… are you moving to North Carolina?"* They weren't thinking about investment opportunities—they were thinking about traditional real estate moves. That's the difference between scarcity thinking and abundance thinking.

But there was one person who kept coming back to me with questions. It was my girlfriend, who is still my girlfriend today, five years later. At first, she was skeptical. She looked at what I was doing and asked, *"Do you really think you can live your dream life by investing in real estate?"*

And without hesitation, I told her, *"Yes. Absolutely."*

I had studied BiggerPockets, followed Brandon Turner's strategies, and fully believed that even if you start slow, if you double your properties every year, you can build real wealth. But believing in something yourself is one thing. Getting someone else to believe it and take action isn't as easy.

My girlfriend wasn't happy with her 401(k) at the time. She watched it grow, but not at the rate she expected. Like so many people, she felt trapped. That's when I showed her a better way. We used The Abundant Wallet Method to free up extra capital. Instead of letting her money sit in a 401(k) with slow returns, we pulled money from her whole life insurance policy and redirected it into real estate investments. She started seeing real cash flow in just a few years and stopped feeling "stuck." Then, we took it a step further.

She had equity in one of her properties that was just sitting there. So, we leveraged that equity to invest in an asset producing 20% returns. That's definitely not something you get from a 401(k) or a traditional retirement account. And for her, that was a huge breakthrough. Once she saw what was possible, she started thinking bigger.

She was changing jobs, which meant she could finally tap into her old 401(k). Instead of just rolling it into another slow-growing fund, we took a different approach. We rolled it into an annuity, which will grow for 10 years. Once she retires, she can start taking distributions. This move gave her far more control over her financial future.

Her story is just one example of what happens when you shift your thinking. Since then, I've helped many others do the same—rethink their 401(k)s, explore alternative financial vehicles, and realize that there is more out there than they ever imagined.

Most people accept the default path—work, save, retire, and hope for the best. But when you take a step back and start questioning the system, you see that there are smarter, faster ways to build wealth.

It all starts with shifting your mindset.

KEY TAKEAWAYS

⮑ A scarcity mindset keeps you stuck in fear and limitation, but shifting to an abundance mindset opens doors to opportunities, growth, and financial freedom.

⮑ Comparing your early progress to someone else's success only holds you back—focus on your own journey, get the reps in, and trust that momentum will increase over time.

⮑ Following the herd usually leads to average results; questioning conventional wisdom and learning from top performers can reveal smarter, faster paths to wealth.

⮑ Financial education is the key to breaking free from limiting beliefs. When you understand how money really works, you can control your financial future.

⮑ True financial independence comes from investing in income-producing assets and thinking beyond traditional retirement plans, allowing you to build long-term wealth on your terms.

CHAPTER TWO

THE TRUTH ABOUT TRADITIONAL ADVICE

Most people assume that their 401(k) is the ultimate retirement vehicle, but it wasn't initially designed for retirement at all. It was meant to match pensions that some organizations had back in the 1970s, but over time, it evolved into something entirely different—something that might not be in your best interest.

To understand how we got here, we have to go back to 1973 when President Nixon took the dollar off the gold standard. That move made money inherently less valuable, and as a result, employers started looking for ways to shift the responsibility of retirement savings away from pensions and onto employees. That's where the ERISA Act came in, offering incentives for employers to contribute to retirement accounts. By the early 1980s, the 401(k) had become the standard.

But Ted Benna, the so-called "father" of the 401(k), never intended it to be used the way it is today. In fact, he's disturbed by what it has become. The hidden fees, the salary reductions, and the limits on how much you can contribute? Those weren't supposed to be part of the equation.

One of the biggest issues with 401(k)s is the fees that aren't always obvious. You're charged for management, administration, and transactions, all of which eat away at your savings. And because your money is tied up in market-driven funds, many of which have a vested interest in keeping you invested, you might not even realize how much you're losing.

Then there's the contribution limit. You're limited to contributing around $20,000–$25,000 per year. If your goal is true financial freedom, how far will that get you? If this was truly a retirement plan, why would there be a cap on how much you can put in? The government isn't limiting how much money you can spend on groceries, a house, or a car. But suddenly, there are restrictions when it comes to saving for your future.

Another major limitation of traditional retirement plans is taxes. Taxes are killing our growth, and I believe they're only going to get worse. You might contribute to your 401(k) pre-tax, which feels like a win up front. But when you retire and start withdrawing that money, you're hit with income taxes—often at a higher rate than you expected.

And don't forget the penalties. If you want to access your own money before the age of 59½, you're hit with an early withdrawal penalty. That's proof right there that you don't really own your retirement savings the way you think you do. If you have to wait until a certain age to access your own money, who really controls it?

I'm not the only one saying this. In *Money: Master the Game*, Tony Robbins calls the 401(k) "the biggest money heist in American history." That sounds extreme, but it makes sense when you step back and look at the system. The fees, the restrictions, and the fact that so many people's retirements are tied up in a system they don't fully understand are all by design.

The Psychology of False Comfort

So, why do so many people still believe in these traditional retirement plans? It comes down to psychology. When 401(k)s were first introduced, they were designed to mimic pensions— the gold standard of retirement security at the time. Back then, if you worked for a company for 30 years, you'd retire with a pension that paid you for life.

However, pensions and 401(k)s are not the same:

- A pension is a guaranteed income for life.
- A 401(k) is a savings account tied to the stock market with no guarantees.

When companies started moving away from pensions, the 401(k) was the next best thing. People accepted it because it was the only widely available option, not the best one. Over time, this became the norm. We've been conditioned to believe that it must be the right thing to do if everyone's doing it.

I read an article not too long ago that ranked countries based on the quality of their retirement systems. The U.S. wasn't even in the top 20. Countries like Denmark have systems that allow people to build real, sustainable retirement plans that are structured differently from our contribution-based model. Seeing how other countries prioritize retirement security in ways we don't is eye-opening.

Here's another thing to think about: when you have a pension, you're vested after a certain period, and when you retire, you receive a lump sum or guaranteed payments. That's real security. But with a 401(k), you're at the mercy of the market, contribution limits, and government regulations.

You can roll over your 401(k) into another account when you switch jobs, but the rules are the same everywhere you go. It's like the difference between working for yourself and working for someone else—there's always going to be limitations when you're not in complete control. Don't confuse familiarity with security. Just because traditional retirement strategies are common doesn't mean they're effective.

The Biggest Misconceptions About Government-Controlled Retirement Plans

One of the biggest myths people believe about plans like 401(k)s and IRAs is the magic of compound interest. You've probably heard the famous quote attributed to Einstein: *"Compound interest is the eighth wonder of the world."* The idea that your money can make money and then that money makes even more money is an attractive concept. The truth is that compound interest isn't as magical as it seems when you look at the actual numbers.

I shared an example in the first chapter about a woman who maxed out her IRA. She contributed $65,000 over ten years, and thanks to compound interest, she earned an additional $35,000. Some people might look at that and think, *"Hey, that's pretty good!"* But $35,000 over ten years isn't exactly life-changing. What's even more frustrating is that this kind of return could've been achieved in a fraction of the time with a true wealth-building strategy. I've seen investors make that same amount—or more—in as little as six months to a year, flipping houses. In fact, I'm currently working on a house flip in Texas that's projected to deliver a similar return in a much shorter time frame.

If you're a late starter like me, compound interest returns aren't going to help you catch up. The problem is people get so mesmerized by the phrase "compound interest" that they forget to ask the important questions: *What are the actual returns? How does it align with my financial goals? Is it helping me build wealth, or is it just helping me save a little more?* 401(k)s and IRAs aren't wealth-building tools. They're just advanced savings accounts. You can make some money with them, especially if the market performs well. But you're just saving and hoping that the market will do the heavy lifting for you.

Another common belief is that the key to success with these

plans is to "stay in it for the long game." You'll hear people say, *"It's not a sprint; it's a marathon,"* or they'll reference Warren Buffett, pointing out that the stock market has averaged around 10% growth over the last decade.

Just because something grows over time doesn't mean it's the best strategy.

I have friends who've made good money in the market, and that's great for them. But for me, the volatility isn't worth the stress. Staying in the market for the "long game" sounds wise on the surface, but it's often just an excuse to ignore the fact that there might be smarter strategies out there. You don't have to settle for slow growth if there are ways to win quicker and with less risk.

Breaking Free from the Accumulation Trap

Traditional financial advice is all about saving, saving, saving— hoarding money in retirement accounts and hoping it grows over time. As Garrett Gunderson puts it in his books, accumulation is just the first step. The real question is: *What is that money doing for you? Is it growing passively? Is it generating income? Is it being reinvested to create more wealth?*

If not, you're missing out. Inflation eats away at stagnant savings, and low interest rates in traditional accounts barely keep you afloat. That's why I focus on putting my money into assets that generate returns through cash flow, equity growth, or both.

One of my biggest realizations was that I didn't have to trade time for money. When I started my financial independence journey, I thought the key to success was working harder and using my skills to earn more. But then I discovered the power of passive and semi-passive income.

If you're just now realizing that traditional retirement planning might not be enough, the first step is simple: start questioning everything. For years, many people, especially Baby Boomers, have been taught the so-called "three-pronged approach" to retirement: relying on Social Security, private savings, and investments. This strategy may have worked for previous generations, but times have changed. Social Security, once considered a stable pillar of retirement income, is now uncertain, its future hanging in the balance as economic pressures mount. Private savings, especially in low-interest savings or checking accounts, barely keep pace with inflation, meaning that every dollar saved is quietly losing value over time. While promising on the surface, investments often fall into the same molds of volatile markets and restrictive government-controlled plans like 401(k)s and IRAs.

Real wealth comes from ownership. That's why I chose real estate. With real estate, you get:

- **Cash Flow:** Regular income from rental properties.
- **Equity Growth:** Your asset appreciates over time.
- **Tax Benefits:** Deductions and incentives that help you keep more of your money.

With real estate—or any income-producing asset—you're not just sitting around, crossing your fingers that the market treats you kindly. Your money is actively working for you every single day (even while you sleep), allowing you to pivot when opportunities arise, invest in what makes sense for you (not what's dictated by government rules), and grow your money without falling victim to emotional market swings, excessive taxes, or liquidity restrictions. Because at the end of the day, wealth isn't just about numbers—it's about the life those numbers allow you to live.

KEY TAKEAWAYS

- ⮑ The 401(k) was never designed to be the ultimate retirement plan; it evolved from a system meant to supplement pensions. It now carries hidden fees, contribution limits, and tax burdens restricting financial freedom.

- ⮑ Traditional retirement plans give the illusion of security, but in reality, they limit control over your own money with government-imposed rules, penalties, and market dependency.

- ⮑ Compound interest, often touted as a wealth-building strategy, delivers underwhelming results compared to more active investment strategies like real estate or business ventures.

- ⮑ Relying solely on the outdated "three-pronged approach" of Social Security, private savings, and investments isn't enough today. These strategies often fail to outpace inflation and rising living costs.

- ⮑ Real wealth comes from ownership—investing in income-producing assets like real estate provides cash flow, equity growth, tax benefits, and the freedom to control your financial future without relying on volatile markets or restrictive retirement plans.

CHAPTER THREE

WHAT ARE YOU SPENDING YOUR MONEY ON?

IF YOU'RE READING THIS BOOK, CHANCES ARE YOU WANT TO build wealth and make your money work for you. That's exactly why this chapter is so important—it's time to reflect on where your money is going. Are you spending on things that set you up for long-term financial success? Or are you putting your money into liabilities that won't serve you in the long run?

If you want to take control of your financial future and start seeing real results, your money should go in three key areas:

1. Invest in Yourself

The best investment you can make is in yourself. Education, self-improvement, and mentorship will accelerate your growth and open up opportunities you never thought possible. This could mean attending seminars, webinars, or workshops or even paying for a mentor to guide you. If you're stepping into new territory, learning from someone who's already been there will speed up your progress significantly. The more knowledge and skills you acquire, the more valuable you become, and that translates to higher earning potential.

2. Buy Assets That Put Money Back in Your Pocket

We've discussed income-producing assets before, which are crucial to financial freedom. The goal should be to own assets that cover all your expenses—and then some. When your investments pay your bills, you've reached a level of financial independence where you can truly enjoy life on your terms.

Maybe you've started your own business or built a portfolio of rental properties or other passive income streams. Whatever the case, the key is to shift from spending money on things that depreciate to putting money into assets that grow and generate cash flow.

3. Prioritize Experiences Over Things

You'll always remember an experience. But material things come and go.

For years, I fell into the trap of spending on things that gave me instant gratification—cars, clothes, gadgets. It was all about keeping up with the Joneses. But those things were liabilities. They weren't putting money in my pocket; they were draining it.

Once I shifted my mindset to one of abundance, I stopped feeling the need to impress others with what I owned. Instead, I focused on relationships, travel, and meaningful experiences— the things that last a lifetime. Now, when I do buy something, it's my income-producing assets that pay for it—not my hard-earned cash.

Conducting a Spending Audit

There are only two basic ways to improve your financial situation: make more money or spend less. It's that simple. To become financially self-sufficient, you must accurately understand how much is coming in and going out.

Many people live in the moment—they check their bank account, see money in there, and think they're fine. But when you step back and look at the big picture, you start to see trends. Maybe you're eating out too much, or your subscription services are piling up. If you don't take control of your spending, it will control you. But when your income consistently exceeds your expenses month after month, that's when you know you're on your way to financial independence.

Forming a habit takes 60 to 90 days, so keep a close eye on your expenses. You have to be disciplined and make sure you're being a good steward of your money, not just spending for the sake of spending.

How to Conduct an Effective Spending Audit

A spending audit doesn't have to be complicated, but it does require some effort and consistency. Here's a process that has worked for me:

1. Use a Tracking Tool

Start by monitoring your spending with a budgeting app or spreadsheet. Seeing your month-over-month trends in different spending categories will show you exactly where your money is going.

2. Cut Unnecessary Expenses

Look for the frivolous expenses that aren't adding real value to your life.

- Do you actually watch that cable bundle for which you're paying $150–$200? I cut mine years ago, and now I use Netflix and Prime—it's way cheaper.

- What about that gym membership? If you're not going regularly, that $25–$30 per month is money down the drain.
- Instead of buying coffee or eating out all the time, start making your own at home and put the savings toward something more meaningful.

3. Check Your Insurance Rates Every Six Months

Whether it's auto, home, or renter's insurance, providers constantly adjust rates. Every six months, I check for better deals. Tools like the Jerry app make it easy to compare rates.

4. Plan for Recurring Expenses with Sinking Funds

One of the best financial habits I've learned is setting aside money in advance for predictable expenses.

- Christmas comes at the same time every year, so why wait until December to scramble for gifts? If you set aside money in the first or second quarter, you'll already have what you need.
- The same applies to annual expenses like property taxes, vacations, or back-to-school shopping. Having a sinking fund eliminates the last-minute financial stress.

5. Use the Debt Snowball Method

Different debt repayment strategies exist, but the Debt Snowball Method worked best for me. Instead of focusing on high-interest debts (like the Avalanche Method does), I started with my smallest debt first. Paying off those small wins quickly built momentum and helped me get out of debt faster.

6. Build Up Your Savings (Preferably in a High-Yield Account)

Saving money is great, but saving in a high-yield savings account is even better. My high-yield account is earning close to 5% interest, meaning my money is working for me—without me lifting a finger.

The Hidden Money Leaks in Your Daily Spending

When people think about cutting expenses, they often focus on the small things we discussed above, like skipping a coffee. But in reality, the most significant financial drains are usually the ones that go unnoticed.

One of the largest expenses people take on is their mortgage or rent. Many of us end up paying more than necessary, tying up money that could be used for investments or other wealth-building opportunities. A more strategic approach would be to ensure that your home is an asset that fits within a broader financial plan rather than an expense that limits future possibilities.

Dining out is another silent budget killer. I know this first-hand because I used to spend way too much on restaurant meals before I made a conscious shift toward cooking at home. Eating out seems harmless at the moment, but the costs add up fast. I know a couple who spends $3,000 a month on dining out for their family of five. That's $36,000 a year that could have been used for a down payment on an investment property or redirected toward financial growth instead of being spent on food that's here today and gone tomorrow.

Another major expense that drains people financially is constantly upgrading cars. Many people feel the urge to buy a new vehicle just because their current one is a few years old. But a car loses value the second you drive it off the lot. I personally keep my cars for as long as they run, even if they need occasional repairs. I drive a 2017 model right now, and it suits me just fine. Since I work from home, I don't feel the need to impress anyone with a new car, and I'd rather put that money toward assets that generate income instead of taking on a hefty monthly car payment.

Subscriptions are another sneaky way money slips through the cracks. Many people don't realize how much they're spending on services they barely use. Whether it's a gym membership that never gets used or multiple streaming platforms stacking up, these costs can quietly eat away at a budget. I know people who subscribe to every streaming service imaginable—Netflix,

Hulu, Disney+, HBO Max, and more—without realizing they're spending over $100 a month to have access to entertainment they may not even watch regularly. A simple spending audit can reveal how much money is wasted on these recurring charges, allowing you to cut back on what isn't adding value.

Personal grooming and cosmetic expenses are another area where people can save. While self-care is important, some costs can be minimized or eliminated with some creativity. For example, I haven't been to a barber in five years because my girlfriend cuts my hair. While a $20 haircut every few weeks might not seem like much, those small amounts add up over time. Salon services like highlights and treatments can be even more expensive. People spend thousands of dollars on cosmetic procedures without considering long-term financial trade-offs. While everyone has different priorities, it's worth asking whether these expenses are necessary or if they're just another form of impulse spending.

Aligning Your Spending with Your Financial Goals

There's no single formula for financial success. Your spending should reflect your personal goals and values. The key is to be intentional with your money rather than impulsive. That means having a clear plan for where you want to go financially and ensuring that every dollar you spend moves you closer to that goal.

The first step is writing down your financial goals, both short-term and long-term. The more specific you are, the easier it becomes to create a plan that aligns with them. Are you saving for a vacation? Hoping to buy a house in the next few years? Working toward financial independence? Whatever your goals may be, putting them in writing gives them structure and allows you to allocate your money wisely. For example, if you're planning a $10,000 family vacation a year from now, waiting until the last minute and scrambling to find the money will only create stress. Start setting aside a little each month, making it much easier to reach your goal without disrupting your finances.

A helpful framework for managing spending is the 50/30/20 rule. Under this model, half of your income goes toward necessities like housing, food, and transportation. Another 30% is allocated to personal wants, such as dining out, entertainment, and hobbies. The remaining 20% is for savings, investments, and long-term financial goals. That final 20% is where wealth-building happens. The more disciplined you are about setting aside money for the future, the faster you'll achieve financial freedom.

For some people, trimming expenses isn't enough to create financial momentum.

Increasing your income becomes the next logical step if you've already cut back and still aren't reaching your goals. I've been there myself—when I was aggressively working to pay off debt and build wealth, I picked up side hustles like DoorDash and Uber Eats. These temporary income streams helped me stay on track until I transitioned into real estate, which completely changed my financial outlook.

Sometimes, the fastest way to earn more money isn't through a side hustle but by changing jobs. Many people don't realize that switching companies can result in a significant pay increase—often $20,000 to $30,000 more for doing the same work. This can be a powerful way to accelerate your income if you're in a high-demand industry. For those who work remotely, applying for positions with West Coast-based companies can also result in higher salaries.

Another effective strategy for increasing financial security is finding ways to monetize skills you already have. If people frequently ask for your help with website development, consulting, or another area of expertise—that's a sign of a marketable skill. Turning something you enjoy into an income stream can be one of your most rewarding financial moves.

If homeownership is one of your financial goals, ensuring a strong credit score is necessary for securing a favorable mortgage rate. One simple credit-building strategy I personally used was an app called Self. This two-year program allows you to make small monthly payments, which are reported to the credit bureaus. Over time, this consistent payment history helps boost your credit score. At the end of the program, you get your money back, making it a win-win. I used this method and saw my credit score increase by 80 points, making qualifying for better financial opportunities much easier.

From Cutting Expenses to Building Wealth

I could share plenty of client success stories, but honestly, my own financial transformation is the best example I can give. For years, I lived paycheck to paycheck, caught in a cycle where my income seemed to disappear as quickly as I earned it. I wasn't reckless, but I was spending without much strategy. That changed the moment I started viewing every financial decision as an investment in my future.

The first thing I did was eliminate unnecessary expenses. I switched to a cheaper insurance plan, cut my cable subscription, and stopped spending money on things that didn't add long-term value to my life. I also traded in my more expensive car for a reliable, lower-cost vehicle with no car payment. All of these changes drastically reduced my monthly expenses, freeing up cash that I could put to better use.

Once I broke free from living paycheck to paycheck, I was able to save 40% of my income—something I never thought would be possible before. But instead of letting that money sit idly, I followed The Abundant Wallet Method, using my savings to invest in assets that generate returns. Just recently, I invested $50,000 into a 61-unit apartment complex in Florissant, Missouri, a deal we closed on in February 2025. This wasn't a one-time move either—this year, we anticipate selling two more commercial properties and reinvesting the profits into new opportunities.

Creating a Spending Plan
for Financial Freedom

For many people, the idea of auditing their spending and making financial changes feels overwhelming. Talking about money, especially budgeting, often carries a negative connotation. That's why I prefer to call it a spending plan. One of the most effective ways to take control of your finances is through zero-based budgeting, where every dollar has a job to do. But you don't have to master it overnight. Take things one step at a time. Start by simply tracking your expenses—even if it's just on a spreadsheet—to get a clearer picture of where your money is going. An excellent method I learned from Dave Ramsey is the envelope system, where you allocate cash into different spending categories. Once an envelope is empty, you stop spending in that category. This kind of hands-on approach forces you to be more conscious about your financial decisions and makes overspending a lot harder.

Automating fixed expenses can also make managing your finances easier. Rent, insurance, and loan payments should be made on autopay, so you don't have to think about them. Variable costs like groceries and gas will fluctuate, but simply budget for them and stay aware of your spending. Over time, these financial habits will create more breathing room in your budget, allowing you to build wealth and gain true financial freedom.

Always think with the end in mind and write down your financial goals. Studies show that 42% of people who write down their goals are more likely to achieve them. At the start of every year, I list what I want to accomplish, personally and professionally. Every month, I review and adjust those goals to stay on track. Keeping them top of mind ensures that my money is always working toward something meaningful.

The goal shouldn't be to stop spending altogether—it's to

spend wisely. Buying things you enjoy is okay, but make sure they align with your financial plan. Be intentional. Avoid impulse purchases. Redirect wasteful spending into investments and assets that will put money back in your pocket. This process requires patience, adjustments, and persistence, but once you master it, you'll be in full control of your money, your future, and your freedom.

KEY TAKEAWAYS

⮑ The way you spend your money determines your financial future. Invest in yourself, buy assets that generate income, and prioritize meaningful experiences over material things.

⮑ Conducting a spending audit helps you take control of your finances by identifying unnecessary expenses, cutting waste, and reallocating money toward wealth-building opportunities.

⮑ Hidden money leaks, such as excessive dining out, frequent car upgrades, and unused subscriptions, can silently drain your budget. Small changes in these areas can lead to big financial gains.

⮑ Align your spending with your financial goals by following a structured plan like the 50/30/20 rule, setting aside money for planned expenses, and ensuring every dollar works toward long-term stability.

⮑ Financial freedom isn't about restricting yourself—it's about being intentional, eliminating waste, and using your money strategically to create lasting wealth.

PART TWO

THE ABUNDANT WALLET BLUEPRINT

CHAPTER FOUR

THE ABUNDANT WALLET METHOD

IF YOU'RE LOOKING FOR A WAY TO MAKE YOUR MONEY WORK FOR you without dealing with the ups and downs of the stock market or the low returns of a traditional bank account, The Abundant Wallet Method is a middle-ground solution. It offers better growth potential than a savings account but is not as unpredictable as investing in stocks.

I've been using this method for the past four years, and it's transformed how I manage my money. I didn't start out knowing all the details, but as I learned and pivoted, I saw how powerful this approach could be. What started as a simple way to put money aside for real estate has become a system allowing me to act as my own bank—funding deals, growing wealth, and controlling my financial future.

When I first got into this, I had no idea what Nelson Nash had created with his banking concept, nor did I realize how I could customize it for today's world. I was just trying to free up some extra money for real estate deals. My approach was pretty basic:

- I had a life insurance policy at $500 a month.
- I also had an Indexed Universal Life (IUL) policy at $300 a month.
- Altogether, I was putting in $800 per month.

After a year and a half, I had about $7,500 in my life insurance policy and around $2,000 in my IUL, for a total of roughly $10,000. That's not bad, considering I was just testing the waters.

At the end of 2022, I realized that I could use this policy as my own bank. That changed everything. Instead of saving money, I saw how to leverage it to fund more real estate deals. By that point, I had already paid off all my personal debt, so I wanted to go all in. I increased my contributions significantly. I started putting in $3,000 a month (roughly $36,000 a year). This was way more than I'd ever done before, but I was committed to making my money work for me. When I had enough extra income from a new policy, real estate sale, or other distributions (typically $100,000 or more), I would front-load it as a lump sum to open new policies. I don't just let it sit there. I leverage it for income-producing assets like real estate.

After four years, here's what I've built:

- I own 9 to 10 properties and counting.
- I've accumulated about $500,000 in assets under management.
- I just rinse and repeat—keep reinvesting until I can completely replace my income.

I now have complete control over my finances. No relying on banks, no stock market stress—just a predictable, strategic way to grow wealth. And the best part? Anyone can do this.

The Abundant Wallet Method isn't just for the wealthy. It works for anyone who is smart with their financial choices and lives below their means. Even if you're making less than six figures, you can still apply this method if you have money you can set aside to grow.

The Key Principles of the Abundant Wallet Method

The Abundant Wallet Method is built around a highly specialized cash value vehicle that provides liquidity, stability, and long-term wealth accumulation. What sets it apart from other financial approaches is that it eliminates reliance on traditional banks and removes unnecessary barriers like credit checks or pay stubs.

Think about most retirement accounts. They're tied to the government and banks, meaning you don't decide how much you contribute, how much you can withdraw, or even when you can access your own money. That never sat right with me. You should have total control over your finances, including how much you put in, when you take it out, and how you use it.

Now you can be the bank. You set the terms. You decide how to use your money, whether investing in real estate, business opportunities, or other wealth-building strategies.

Here's why this method works so well:

★ **Financial Security & Generational Wealth:** This system creates a family bank that can be passed down. Your heirs will benefit from the assets you've built and the financial foundation you've set up for them.

★ **Cash Flow and Liquidity:** Your money stays liquid, meaning you can access it anytime without penalties or restrictions.

★ **Legacy Protection:** Instead of just saving money, you're building a financial legacy that outlives you.

★ **Tax Advantages:** Unlike other investment vehicles, the Abundant Wallet Method offers tax efficiencies that help you keep more of what you earn.

★ **Guaranteed Growth:** You're not gambling in the stock market or waiting for real estate to appreciate. Your money grows predictably over time, giving you a solid foundation.

Honestly, I didn't set out to develop a system. I just needed a way to build wealth efficiently without spending hours managing investments. I still have a W-2 job, plus my real estate investing company and financial services business. Time is my biggest challenge.

I came up with the Abundant Wallet Method because I know many people are stuck in the rat race, just like me. I wanted something efficient, easy to use, and didn't require constant oversight. Of course, there was a lot of trial and error in the beginning. I had to pivot and adjust to perfect the system for my own needs. But now it's repeatable. It works for anyone who is willing to keep an open mind and commit to maximizing cash value and returns. Most importantly, it means your money works for you even while you sleep. You're no longer babysitting investments, reacting emotionally to market shifts, or making decisions based on headlines.

I was skeptical when I first started, too. But over time, I realized this is one of the most effective wealth-building tools available. And now, I want to share it with as many people as possible so you can stop trading time for money and start living on your terms.

How to Get Started with the Abundant Wallet Method

Many ask me, "How do I start using the Abundant Wallet Method?" And that's a great question. The process isn't complicated, but it's important to go through each step correctly to maximize your returns, maintain liquidity, and build wealth on your terms.

I recently hired a business coach, and one of the first things they asked me was, "What are you offering people?" That got me thinking because there's a big difference between marketing something and actually offering a straightforward, step-by-step process. So, here's the breakdown of exactly how the Abundant Wallet Method works and how you can start using it today.

Step 1: Wealth Roadmap
Financial Analysis & Custom Plan

Everything starts with a thorough financial analysis. We look at:

- Your current income, expenses, and savings habits.
- Where your money is currently going.
- The gaps in your wealth-building strategy.

Once we have that baseline, we customize a plan based on what's most important to you:

- Higher income up front? There's a plan for that.
- Higher returns on the back end? We can design it that way.
- More security and stability? No problem.

This isn't a one-size-fits-all strategy. It's specifically designed to help you build wealth the way you want.

Step 2: Asset Activation
Implementing the Abundant Wallet Method

After finalizing the best plan for you, we will implement the Abundant Wallet Method. This usually takes three to six weeks to secure everything with compliance, but in some cases, it can move faster. Then, once the method is officially assigned to you, it's time to start using it.

As you begin generating income, you can start front-loading your wealth-building vehicles.

Here's where a major shift happens:

- Instead of keeping money in a regular bank account, where it earns next to nothing, you store it in a financial warehouse constantly working for you.
- You're not limited to just one policy. You can create multiple financial vehicles that align with your goals.
- You get best-in-class financial products from one or multiple carriers, ensuring you always have access to the highest returns and best liquidity options available.

Step 3: Strategic Growth
The Power of a Whole Life Policy with Cash Value

At the core of the Abundant Wallet Method is a properly structured whole life insurance policy that has cash value:

- You intentionally overfund the policy. That extra money goes straight into your cash value.

- On average, you're earning 5-10% per year. That's guaranteed growth, not market speculation.
- You can borrow against it anytime. If you have a lump sum, you can access funds immediately. If you're contributing monthly, you might need to build up before borrowing, but your money always works for you.

There are also different structures depending on your preference:

- Some plans let you borrow up to 90% immediately.
- Others build slower but provide more income after the 5th or 10th year.
- Some require you to leave 20% in as security, but it still grows as you use it.

No matter which structure you choose, your money is never sitting idle.

Rinse and Repeat

Once you start using the Abundant Wallet Method, you don't stop. You keep reinvesting, growing, and leveraging your financial vehicles repeatedly.

- You can open new policies and expand your financial warehouse when you generate a lump sum.

- You no longer have to rely on banks when building your private banking system.
- Over time, you replace your income, secure your financial future, and pass down generational wealth.

The best part is scalability. Whether you're starting with $500 a month or $50,000, it works the same way, and over time, it completely transforms how you think about wealth.

Rules to Live By When Considering The Abundant Wallet Method

This financial vehicle is not for everyone. It is not a get-rich scheme. It's a strategy that builds wealth over time, not a magic button where you start cash flowing from day one unless you put a significant lump sum in.

That said, I want to be transparent about how this works on the back end. If you're paying a month-to-month premium that is within your budget, it may take several years before the cash accumulates significantly.

- These policies are relatively complex. Accordingly, you will need to understand how loan interest and surrender charges apply. That will be key to the proper management of your investment.

- If you cancel the policy early or have a lapse where the policy gets canceled, you will lose a large portion of the cash value accumulation.

- When you borrow money from your policy, paying the loan back will enable you to continue borrowing as appropriate and ensure that there is enough left over in the policy to cover insurance costs. Likewise, when you take loans from the policy, you are reducing your death benefit and cash value.

- Beware of the MEC Line (Modified Endowed Contract), where you fund the policy with too much money too quickly—you could lose your tax advantages. If total premiums paid, usually within the first 7 years, exceed the amount allowed, this is a taxable event from an IRS perspective.

- Utilizing tax code 7702 allows you to take advantage of a policy using cash value, where there are two accounts—one for insurance and one for cash value. The insurance account pays for the death benefit and policy fees. The cash value account enables you to earn interest on the balance, which is based on the extra premiums paid.

A Real-Life Transformation

One of the best parts about sharing the Abundant Wallet Method is how it changes people's lives. Last year, I worked with a client who stood out because his journey shows how powerful this method can be, even for someone already making wise financial decisions.

He was a 45-year-old paralegal from New York. He didn't have kids or a wife; he just had a strong work ethic and a desire to make his money work harder for him. Like many people, he had a 401(k) that felt out of his control and an Indexed Universal Life (IUL) policy that wasn't delivering the returns he wanted. He wasn't looking to take big risks, but he did want better returns and more flexibility over his finances.

After discussing his options, he realized his existing plans weren't serving him the way he wanted. He decided to redirect his 401(k) and IUL contributions into the Abundant Wallet Method, committing to putting $1,000 per month into it. It was an easy choice with higher returns and the security of never losing money.

What made this decision so effective for him was the sense of control he gained over his money. No longer was he at the mercy of stock market fluctuations, hoping for a good year. His returns immediately improved compared to his traditional plans, and even the highest-yield savings accounts couldn't compete with what he was earning. More than that, he now had an emergency fund that didn't just sit in a bank earning little to no interest—it was actively growing yet still accessible whenever he needed it.

Invest in Yourself

Too often, people dismiss financial strategies because they aren't widely known or don't align with what the masses are doing. Maybe they hear negative opinions, or someone calls it a scam. The truth is, many people who criticize these tools have their own agenda, or they're just stuck in their old ways. You have to be willing to look beyond the mainstream narrative and think for yourself. These aren't just financial tactics—they're investments in yourself. And if you refuse to consider them, you might be missing something that could completely change your financial trajectory.

The Abundant Wallet Method is about control, security, and freedom. Unlike traditional financial plans that leave you at the mercy of banks, the government, or the stock market, this method ensures that you are in charge of your wealth. Your money grows consistently without market risk. You won't lose a dime in an economic downturn. And you'll benefit from tax-free, continuously compounding wealth.

The living benefits allow you to access your capital anytime, without the bank's permission and without having to wait until you are 65. That means you can fund new opportunities, invest in real estate, or expand your business without selling stocks, pulling from retirement accounts, or taking financial hits from early withdrawal penalties.

It's also a generational wealth strategy. Your money is protected and transferred tax-free to your heirs. There's no probate, no legal battles, and no government interference. You decide how your wealth is structured and preserved for generations to come.

Building wealth doesn't have to mean chasing stock market gains or tying up your money in restrictive retirement accounts. The Abundant Wallet Method allows you to grow, leverage, and reinvest your money with purpose, whether you're just starting out or looking to optimize your existing wealth-building strategy. The key is to think differently, take action, and stay committed to making your money work for you. When you do, financial freedom becomes a reality within your reach.

KEY TAKEAWAYS

- The Abundant Wallet Method provides a stable way to create wealth. It offers better returns than a traditional savings account while avoiding the volatility of the stock market.

- By leveraging a properly structured whole life insurance policy with cash value, you can create a personal banking system that keeps your money working for you, providing liquidity and financial security.

- The method is scalable. Whether you start with a few hundred dollars a month or make significant contributions, it works the same way over time to replace income and build generational wealth.

- Success with this method doesn't require taking risks. Simply make strategic financial decisions, stay committed, and continuously reinvest to create lasting financial freedom.

CHAPTER FIVE

BUILD WEALTH BEYOND SAVING: ASSETS THAT WORK FOR YOU

You can't save your way to wealth. Many people believe if they just put money in a savings account and let it sit, they're doing the right thing. But with interest rates at traditional banks being what they are, you're not building wealth—you're actually losing money. Inflation is eating away at it faster than any interest you're earning. Now, don't get me wrong. You need an emergency fund for life's unexpected events. But beyond that, if you want to stop trading time for money, you have to put your money to work.

That's where income-producing assets come in. Assets can

make more money for you than any job ever could. And the best part? They do it while you sleep. For me, that meant real estate. I took two of my properties and put them to work. Together, they generate about $5,800 per month in passive income. That's $70,000 per year before the debt service is paid without me lifting a finger. And that's just from two properties. Imagine scaling that. If I add another two or three properties like that, I can completely replace my income. Once your cash flow/profits supersede your expenses, you are financially independent and don't have to trade time for money if you choose. No more punching a clock. No more rat race!

You might only think about the cash flow from investments, and yeah, that's great; it's money in your pocket every month. But there's something even bigger at play: equity. Over time, those properties appreciate. When you sell, you don't just get back what you put in—you multiply it. That's capital you can reinvest into even bigger deals. It's a snowball effect. The bigger the deals, the bigger the wealth accumulation. Once you have an income-producing asset or even a scalable side business, you can repeat the process over and over again. And each time, you move further away from needing a paycheck and closer to financial independence.

Starting Your Investing Journey: From Saver to Investor

So, how do you go from saving money to investing it? If you've never done it before, it can feel overwhelming. When I first started, I didn't have all the answers either. I had to figure it out as I went. For me, the transition began with a robo-advisor. At the time, I had read enough about 401(k)s, fees, and hidden costs that I knew I didn't want to pay someone a percentage of my money just to manage it. Instead, I used a robo-advisor, an automated investment tool that manages your portfolio based on your preferences.

One example is *Betterment,* which I used when I first started. It let me set my own investment mix, whether I wanted 40% stocks, 60% bonds, or vice versa —and manage it all through an app. No financial advisor was needed.

That was my introduction to investing. But as I got deeper into personal finance, my mindset shifted. At first, I was still a saver at heart. I had most of my money sitting in savings and just a small portion invested. But over time, I started to see the numbers:

- Savings accounts weren't growing my money—they were just holding it.
- Investments, even with ups and downs, were producing real returns.

So, I flipped the script. I went from putting most of my money into savings and just a little into investments to doing the exact opposite. There's no one-size-fits-all answer to where you should begin. It all depends on your personality and risk tolerance. That's why I always recommend:

→ **Taking a risk profile quiz:** This can help you under-stand how comfortable you are with risk and what types of investments might be a good fit.

→ **Diversifying your investments:** Never put all your eggs in one basket. Some investments will grow faster than others, but having a mix protects you from significant losses.

→ **Understanding your timeline:** Some investments take years to grow, while others generate income faster. The key is balancing short-term and long-term plays.

The most important thing is to just get started. Don't let fear or analysis paralysis keep you from building wealth.

Real Estate: The Best Income-Generating Asset for Beginners

If you're just starting and wondering what the best income-generating assets are, you're not alone. Most people who build serious wealth start small and work their way up. That's exactly how I started with real estate. I began with a single-family house, just one property, and built from there. It's a numbers game; you want your rental income to be greater than your mortgage or expenses so you're actually making a profit. If the numbers don't make sense, it's not a good investment.

The coolest thing about real estate investing is that you don't have to do it alone. This is a team business—you have property managers, contractors, and leasing agents who handle most of the work for you. So, while it's not *entirely* passive, it can be semi-passive with the right structure. One great way to get started, especially if you have little capital, is house hacking.

Here's how it works:

- You buy a duplex, triplex, or fourplex.
- You live in one unit and rent out the others.
- Your tenants pay your mortgage, so you're living for free.

That's a fast-track strategy to create wealth because you're reducing your housing costs while generating rental income. And as you scale up—say, moving from a duplex to a triplex or fourplex—you increase your cash flow and spread your risk. Think about it:

- If you own a single-family rental and your tenant moves out, you're making zero income until you find a new renter.
- If you own a fourplex and one tenant moves out, three other tenants still pay you. That means only 25% vacancy instead of 100%.

The more doors you have, the more stability you create. And here's the best part—once you own a property, you can use that income to buy more properties. It's a cycle:

- Buy a rental property.
- Collect rent and build equity.
- Sell or refinance and buy another one.
- Repeat until your cash flow covers all your expenses.

That's how you scale from a side hustle to a full-time wealth-building machine. I own around 10 properties and usually put in five hours a week because I have a team managing them. That's five hours a week for a full-time income—less work than a single shift at most jobs.

The Biggest Misconceptions About Real Estate Investing

When people hear about investing in real estate, they often assume it's easy money—that they'll buy a property, start collecting rent, and instantly become financially free. I've seen many people jump in with unrealistic expectations, and when things don't go exactly as they imagined, they quit and move on to something else. If you want to be successful, you need to know what to expect.

Misconception #1: You Start Making Money on Day One

This is one of the biggest myths in real estate investing. Some people think the moment they close on a property, the money just starts rolling in. That's not reality. Unless you land an absolutely fantastic deal with experienced partners—maybe as a limited partner in syndication where you're not handling operations—you're probably not going to see profits right away.

I'll be the first to tell you that it took me seven months to get my first property, and it wasn't cash-flowing from day one. Not every deal is a home run right out of the gate. You have to be patient. The key is learning, improving, and making more intelligent decisions with every investment.

Misconception #2:
Due Diligence Is Just a Formality

A lot of new investors take the seller's word at face value and that's a mistake. Due diligence is everything.

Here's what you need to double-check before buying:

- ✓ Financials: Get proof of net operating income (NOI) over the past two years.
- ✓ Tenant history: Ensure rent is being paid on time—no exceptions.
- ✓ Property condition: Inspections matter. If there are problems, negotiate concessions from the seller.

You can't just assume everything is in order. You need proof.

Misconception #3:
Walking Away from a Deal is a Failure

You haven't failed if you back out of a bad deal! The truth is, walking away from a bad deal is a win. If the numbers don't make sense, the expenses are too high, and the cash flow isn't there, it's better to walk away now than lose money later. I've walked away from deals before, and I'm sure I will do it again. There are always more deals out there.

Misconception #4:
Real Estate Investing is Emotional

For most people, buying a house is an emotional experience. They imagine living in it, raising a family, and making memories. But when it comes to real estate investing, you have to take the emotion out of it. This isn't about finding your dream home but making smart business decisions. If a deal falls through, it's not personal. If a property doesn't perform well, you adjust and move forward.

Misconception #5:
You Can't Control Property Values

A lot of people think that property appreciation is just luck— that you have to wait for the market to rise before your investment grows in value. That's not true. You can create your own appreciation. This is called forced appreciation, and it's one of the most powerful strategies in real estate.

How Forced Appreciation Works

If your property isn't commanding top market rent, you can increase its value by making improvements:

- Upgrade the floors, cabinets, and countertops.
- Improve the curb appeal.
- Add modern amenities that renters are looking for.

By making these strategic upgrades, you can increase rent and overall property value on your terms. In some ways, forced appreciation is better than compound interest because you control the outcome. You're not waiting for the market—you're actively making your property worth more.

The Most Important Factors to Consider Before Purchasing a Rental Property

There are certain rules and gut checks that can help you avoid costly mistakes when you start your real estate investing journey. I could write an entire book on this (and people have), but I want to break it down into the key things I personally look at before buying a rental property.

1. The 1% Rule

A good rule of thumb for rental property investing is the 1% rule. This means:

- ✓ If you buy a house for $100,000, you should make at least $1,000 monthly rent.
- ✓ If the rent doesn't meet or exceed 1% of the purchase price, the deal might not be worth it.

This isn't a hard rule—different markets have different dynamics—but it's a good gut check to filter out bad deals quickly.

There's great software out there to help you analyze rental prices in any area. Some of my go-to tools are:

- **Rentometer**: Helps you compare rental rates for similar properties.
- **PropStream**: Provides market analysis, property data, and investment insights.

Punch in the zip code, number of bedrooms, and square footage, and you'll get an accurate picture of what rent you can realistically charge.

2. Build the Right Team

I don't know any successful investor who built their portfolio entirely on their own. Real estate is a team sport, and who you have in your corner matters.

- ✓ Talk to multiple lenders: Different lenders offer different products (fix-and-flip loans, buy-and-hold loans, etc.), and comparing them can save you thousands.
- ✓ Qualify and disqualify contractors, property managers, and agents: Interview multiple people; don't just go with the first one you meet.
- ✓ Find a mentor or coach: This is a game-changer. A great mentor will 10x or even 20x your results because they help you avoid rookie mistakes.

Eventually, once you master the process, you won't need an entry-level mentor, but having someone to bounce ideas off of early on is invaluable.

3. Run the Numbers and Get a Second Opinion

One of the biggest mistakes new investors make is not analyzing enough deals. You can't just run the numbers once and assume everything looks good—you need a second and third set of eyes.

- ✓ Join a mastermind or investor group: More experienced investors can help you spot red flags you might miss.
- ✓ Analyze as many deals as possible: Even if you don't buy them, running through the numbers sharpens your skills.
- ✓ Compare multiple properties: If a deal doesn't work, move on to the next—there are always more.

4. Location, Location, Location

A great house in a bad neighborhood is still a bad investment. Before buying, do your research on the area:

- ✓ Check crime rates: You don't want your tenants worrying about safety.
- ✓ Look at school ratings: Even if you're renting to people without kids, homes in good school districts tend to hold value better.

✓ Understand property grading (A, B, C, D neighborhoods):

- **A-class neighborhoods** – Expensive, high-end, great long-term value, but lower cash flow.
- **B-class neighborhoods** – Middle-class, good appreciation, and strong rental demand.
- **C-class neighborhoods** – Older properties, lower-income areas, but higher cash flow potential.
- **D-class neighborhoods** – High crime, lots of vacancies—avoid unless you really know what you're doing.

The best investment strategy I've found is to buy a C-class property in a B or A-class neighborhood. You get it at a lower price, renovate to match the surrounding properties, and watch your rent and equity grow alongside higher-end homes!

When you take these steps, you're not gambling but investing with confidence. And remember—you don't have to be perfect to get started. You just need to get started.

Breaking Old Habits and Embracing New Opportunities

One of the hardest parts of transitioning from a saver to an investor is the mental shift required. If you've spent your whole life being told to put money away, keep it safe, and avoid risk, investing where your money is actively working for you can feel unnatural. It's a complete rewiring of everything you've been taught.

I've known many people who have gone through this transition, and it's never easy. It's not just about learning new financial strategies; it's about letting go of old beliefs. For years, we've been told that debt is bad, that saving for a rainy day is the smartest thing we can do, and that risk is something to avoid. But when you start building wealth, you realize that the right kind of debt can actually make you rich, that saving alone will never create financial freedom, and that taking smart, calculated risks is the only way to grow.

One of the biggest challenges people face in this shift isn't just internal—it's the voices of those around them. I noticed it firsthand when I started investing in real estate. Suddenly, people who had never invested in anything themselves had the strongest opinions. "That's too risky," they'd say. "What if the market crashes? What if tenants stop paying?" It's funny how the loudest voices often belong to people who aren't actually doing the thing they're warning you about.

I realized that the people who are truly building wealth don't spend their time discouraging others—they focus on creating opportunities and sharing what they've learned. That's why surrounding yourself with the right people is crucial. If you want to succeed as an investor, you need to be around others who are doing the same. Finding mentors, joining investment groups, and staying in conversations with experienced investors will give you access to insights and opportunities you won't get from sitting on the sidelines. The truth is, your network is your net worth. If you surround yourself with people who understand wealth-building, you'll think differently, see opportunities more clearly, and gain the confidence to take action.

Building wealth isn't complicated. It's simply consistently putting your money into assets that grow and generate income. The problem is that most people never do it because it feels unfamiliar and intimidating. They assume it's reserved for people with finance degrees or deep industry connections. But the truth is the majority of millionaires—ninety percent of them, according to studies—have been created through real estate investing.

That statistic alone should make you pause. If nearly all self-made millionaires are using one asset class to create their wealth, that's a strong sign that the opportunity is there for anyone willing to learn and take action.

The people who succeed in this game don't quit after one setback. They don't expect their first deal to be perfect. They don't let doubt or fear keep them from moving forward. Every experience—every deal that goes smoothly and every deal that doesn't—teaches something valuable. No two investments are ever exactly alike, but the more you do, the more patterns you recognize and the smarter you become.

Your mindset determines your wealth. If you continue thinking like a saver, you'll always be working for money. If you shift to thinking like an investor, your money will start working for you. The difference between the middle class and the wealthy is what they do with the money they earn.

The more you learn, invest, and surround yourself with the right people, the bigger your opportunities will become. What starts as a single rental property, a single investment, can quickly turn into a portfolio that funds your lifestyle, your dreams, and your legacy.

KEY TAKEAWAYS

➲ Saving alone will not build wealth; inflation will erode savings, and true financial independence comes from income-generating assets that work for you.

➲ Investing in real estate offers both passive income and long-term equity growth, creating a scalable strategy for financial freedom.

➲ Transitioning from a saver to an investor requires a mindset shift—understanding risk, leveraging diversification, and taking action despite fear.

➲ Misconceptions about real estate investing, such as expecting instant profits or neglecting due diligence, can derail success; patience and strategy are key.

➲ Wealth isn't reserved for the ultra-rich. Most self-made millionaires built their wealth through real estate, proving that opportunity exists for anyone willing to learn and take action.

CHAPTER SIX

DON'T LEAVE MONEY ON THE TABLE

You can do many things to improve your financial position—most of them hiding in plain sight. I'm talking about leveraging opportunities people overlook simply because they don't take the time to do a little research or due diligence. Money comes in different forms. It's not just about cash sitting in your bank account. There's the cash value in life insurance (The Abundant Wallet Method), equity in your home, and interest you're paying to banks or other institutions. All of these can be re-evaluated and leveraged differently. But too often, people take the easy route, and that's where money gets left on the table.

One of the biggest mindset shifts I help people make is

looking beyond cost and focusing on value. There's a difference. Too many people get caught up in how cheap or inexpensive something is. But if you're only looking for the lowest price, you might be making decisions that are actually costing you more in the long run. That "cheap" option may be robbing you of a better future.

It's time to open your eyes to possibilities. If you've got time to do a little discovery, you might be surprised by what you find. Get curious. Get smarter. Learn how to make money work harder for you and your family. That's the difference between surviving and truly creating an abundant life.

The Sneaky Ways You're Giving Money Away

Let's discuss some of the most common ways people unknowingly leave money on the table. There are a lot more than most people realize. I'll highlight a few that stand out to me because they're common but avoidable.

First off, paying too much interest to banks. This one's a silent killer. If you're carrying a balance on your credit cards and only making the minimum payments—or just a little more—it's going to take forever to pay those off. That's what we call bad debt. It's not helping you grow. It's holding you back. That money you're sending to credit card companies every month could be going into something much more lucrative that builds wealth instead of draining it.

Another big one is not leveraging your cash value life

insurance. This is a cornerstone of The Abundant Wallet Method. That value is a powerful tool to invest in other deals. If you're not tapping into it strategically, that's money you're letting sit idle while you miss out on opportunities to grow.

Then there's home equity. Most people consider their house a place to live, but it can also be a source of capital that works for you. I've seen people use a home equity line of credit (HELOC) to buy new cars or remodel their homes. Those things might feel important at the moment. But if you're going to leverage money, do it in a way that makes it produce something for you.

I've learned a lot from colleagues and mentors who are ahead of me on this journey. I intentionally surround myself with people smarter than me in certain areas because that pushes me to grow. And one thing I've picked up is how smart people use their equity. They'll take out a line of credit and use that money to invest in real estate or other cash-producing assets. But they don't just borrow the money and hope for the best. They plan for it. They set aside a portion of that money specifically to cover their HELOC payments for the year, so they're not scrambling later. That's strategy. That's discipline. And that's how you turn borrowed money into a tool that works for you.

And as for paying off your house early, I know this might sound controversial, but I don't think that's always the best move. I have tenants covering my mortgage, so why rush to pay it off? Instead, I'd rather use my extra money to invest in other income-producing assets.

Don't forget about your savings, either. Many people leave their money in traditional savings accounts because it's convenient. But right now, high-yield savings accounts are a much better option. If your money's going to sit, it should at least earn something. Otherwise, you're just handing over potential interest earnings.

And finally, taxes. I'm not talking about doing anything shady. There are legal tax strategies to defer taxes or even eliminate them. There are so many good legal loopholes people don't know about because they've never taken the time to learn. But once you understand how the tax game works, you can play it differently and keep a lot more of your money.

Little-Known Tax Strategies That Can Save You Big

One of the things I've spent a lot of time on over the years—just on my own, out of curiosity—is researching tax strategies. I've encountered many tools and advantages that most people never hear about. I haven't used some of these myself yet, but I've recommended them to others.

Let's begin with real estate. If you're selling a property, you can use a 1031 exchange. This lets you defer the taxes on your profit as long as you roll the money into another qualifying property. That can be a huge win when building long-term wealth through real estate.

By this point in the book, you know I'm a fan of cash value life insurance. One reason is that it grows tax-deferred while you're alive and tax-free when it passes to your heirs. That's all backed by Tax Code 7702, and it's a game-changer for building generational wealth in a tax-advantaged way.

Here's another powerful one: Section 72(t) of the tax code. This lets you take penalty-free withdrawals from your retirement accounts—like 401(k)s and IRAs—before you turn 59½. A lot of people think you have to wait until retirement to access that money without penalty, but with this rule, you don't. It can give you more flexibility, especially if you're planning to retire early or just need access to funds.

Another option is the Rule of 55. If you leave your job at age 55 or older, you can withdraw from your current job's 401(k) or 403(b) without the 10% early withdrawal penalty. Here's the catch: you must have left your job, and you can't have another one lined up or on the books. But for the right person, this rule can be a useful way to access funds earlier than you'd expect.

And here's one that I think is especially cool for business owners and real estate investors—a charitable trust. I've seen people use this to their advantage in a big way. If you set up a charitable trust and have that trust own an asset—like a piece of real estate or your business—then you can eliminate the capital gains tax when that asset is sold. That's huge. It's a different route than doing a 1031 exchange, and it could be even better for the right situation.

Taxes don't have to be the enemy. When you understand the rules, you can actually use them to your advantage!

How One Strategy Can Save You Thousands—Or Even Millions

I've seen firsthand how powerful these financial tools can be, especially for real estate investors. One of the best examples is how people leverage the 1031 exchange to save hundreds of thousands—sometimes even millions—of dollars by deferring taxes on property sales.

And we're not talking about small single-family rentals here. I'm talking about big-time deals—commercial properties and large syndications that generate major profits. When these investors sell a property, instead of handing over a considerable chunk of their gains to the IRS, they use a 1031 exchange to defer those capital gains taxes by reinvesting into a new property.

Here's how it works: once you sell your investment property, the clock starts ticking. You have 45 days to identify a new property and 180 days total to close on it. The new property has to be of equal or lesser value, and it has to be an investment property, not something personal like your primary residence. As long as you follow these rules, you can roll over your gains into the new property without paying capital gains tax, at least not yet.

The benefits are:

- Tax deferral, which keeps more cash in your hands to reinvest.
- Wealth building, as your assets grow and compound over time.

- Portfolio diversification, because you can move into different markets or types of properties.
- Estate planning benefits, since you can pass on assets with built-in advantages.

You don't pay those deferred taxes unless you decide to stop investing and sell without reinvesting. But if you stay in the game and keep exchanging up, you keep rolling that tax bill forward, and your wealth keeps building. It makes sense to me. Why write a check to the government now when you could reinvest that money, create more income, and plan your exit on your terms later? These are the kinds of strategies that turn good decisions into great ones.

Are You Actually Winning with Your 401(k)? Maybe Not.

We've discussed how taxes can work in our favor, but what about our 401(k)s? Many people treat their 401(k) like it's set-it-and-forget-it, and honestly, that's one of the biggest mistakes you can make when it comes to your retirement. I don't know if it's the media or just the way we've been conditioned, but most folks think, "If I'm contributing and getting an employer match, I'm doing fine."

If you really want to maximize the benefit, you've got to do more than just contribute. You need a cohesive plan for how that money is being invested. Too many people have no clue which funds they're in—or worse, they trust someone to manage it without even asking questions. And not all advisors are created equal. Some aren't fiduciaries, which means they're not legally required to act in your best interest. That's a problem.

Then, the fees come into play, and this is where people really get blindsided. Most don't read the prospectus or pay attention to how their investments are actually performing. They don't know what fees they're paying or why. But those fees add up, especially the hidden ones that no one tells you about.

Here are just a few types of fees you might be paying without realizing it:

- 12b-1 fees (which are basically marketing fees baked into your fund's cost)
- Investment fees
- Administrative fees
- Individual service fees charged by your provider
- Custodial fees based on how and where your assets are held

The size of your employer's plan, the number of participants, and the provider they've partnered with all affect how much you're being charged. And the more money you contribute, the more these fees can eat into your returns. So, if you think you're doing everything right by putting money in your 401(k), look closer. You might be unknowingly giving away thousands of dollars over time. Read your statements. Know your fees. And make sure your investments are working for you—not just for the companies managing your plan.

From Side Hustles to Passive Income: Start Where You Are

When I started looking for extra money, my mindset wasn't anywhere near where it is today in terms of passive income and long-term financial growth. But I knew one thing—I had debt, and I wanted to get rid of it. So, I started where I could. I got into DoorDash and Uber Eats, and it was a grind, but it worked. It brought in extra cash, and it was a stepping stone.

Later, I started learning more about real estate investing and saw the potential for passive income. When done strategically, real estate is still one of the strongest ways to build long-term wealth. Another one I'm starting to explore is affiliate marketing. I've partnered with people who offer solid products and services; every time someone I refer makes a purchase, I earn a percentage. That's money coming in without having to trade time for it every day.

Other side hustles I've seen work for people include tutoring, coaching, and using technical skills like building websites or setting up e-commerce stores. These are all great ways to generate extra income based on what you already know or can easily learn.

Then there's velocity banking, which involves using the equity in your home to fuel other investments. Again, it's all about making your existing resources work smarter—not just harder—for you. It starts with your mindset. You could be holding yourself back if you're not open to new ideas. You don't have to jump on every opportunity but don't dismiss something just because it's new to you. Use a "trust and verify" approach: learn about it, weigh the pros and cons, research, analyze trends, and study case studies. You might be surprised by what works once you give it a fair shot.

Also, don't quit too soon. I see people start businesses or side hustles, and if they're not making money after a year or two, they give up. Remember that success often comes with time and reps.

Paying It Forward

If there's one action you can take today to begin maximizing your financial resources, it's seeking out mentorship. I wish I had done this earlier in my journey. It's easy to feel overwhelmed by the myriad of strategies and tools available, but finding someone who has navigated these waters successfully can provide clarity and direction.

Sometimes, pride or jealousy can prevent us from reaching out to those who are thriving financially. But setting aside those feelings and genuinely learning from their experiences can be transformative. Whether it's joining a mastermind group, enrolling in a course, or having in-depth conversations with someone you admire, discover the details of their success.

Understand not just what they did but how they did it. By adopting their habits, you position yourself for financial growth. And as you achieve your own success, remember to pay it forward. Help others on their journey, creating a cycle of mentorship and growth.

There are countless avenues to generate additional income streams. Choose paths that align with your interests and passions, making the learning process enjoyable. However, always remember that money is merely a tool. It's not the ultimate goal but a means to achieve broader objectives.

The primary aim should be to assist others. When you selflessly impact as many lives as possible without expecting anything in return, you open yourself to a world of opportunities. In doing so, you achieve abundance and contribute to a more prosperous and compassionate world.

KEY TAKEAWAYS

- There's hidden money all around you—whether in your home equity, life insurance cash value, or high-interest payments—and with the right strategy, you can turn those overlooked resources into tools for wealth building.

- The key isn't finding the cheapest option; it's investing in value and using your resources to create more cash flow, equity, or long-term financial growth.

- Legal tax strategies like 1031 exchanges, cash value life insurance, and charitable trusts can help you keep more of what you earn and grow your wealth faster if you understand how to use them.

- Side hustles and passive income streams, even small ones, can be powerful stepping stones toward financial independence if you stay consistent and strategic.

- Success starts with mentorship. Surround yourself with people who are ahead of you financially, learn from their actions, and then pay it forward to help others rise, too.

PART THREE

BREAK FREE AND CREATE A LEGACY

CHAPTER SEVEN

LEAVE A LEGACY OF ABUNDANCE

Building up wealth, growing businesses, and creating success for yourself is one thing. But it's a costly and generational mistake if you don't take the time to protect that wealth or plan for how it will benefit your family or future family.

I want you to think really long-term here as Stephen Covey talks about starting with the end in mind. That same mind-set should apply to your money. When you start earning and investing your money, you've got to secure and protect it so it keeps working for you, your children, your grandchildren, and beyond like clockwork.

Life is busy. It's tempting to say, "I'll figure out the legacy stuff later." But the truth is, if you don't be intentional and take action now, what you've built could disappear faster than you think. I'm talking about something I've seen over and over again—what I call the two-generation curse.

Here's how it happens: A family makes money, builds a business, invests well, and creates a nice life. But they never put a plan in place to protect that wealth. They never sit down to think about family governance or what it means to leave a legacy that actually lasts. And by the time the second generation is enjoying the fruits of all that hard work, the cash starts to fade. By the third generation? It's often gone.

You can't just scatter your money among your living relatives and hope for the best. That approach almost always leads to the money getting squandered. Instead of creating lasting abundance, all that money ends up funding short-term lifestyles, and then it's gone. The next generation is left to start all over again from scratch.

In order to leave a legacy of abundance, focus on passing down the knowledge that got you there in the first place, such as the decisions you made, the planning you did, and the values you lived by. Those are just as important—if not more important—than the money itself.

When you do it right, your kids, grandkids, and even great-grandkids get a head start to freedom. They get the kind of life where they don't have to struggle the way you might've had to. You can't just hand the cash off and say, "Have fun!" The younger generations need to be guided so they understand what you did and why you did it.

Let me give you a picture of what I mean—two families, two different outcomes.

Family One wasn't as wealthy as Family Two, but they were smart. They preserved what they had and set it up correctly. They used cash value life insurance to create a powerful family bank. This allowed their wealth to keep growing and flowing across generations. They left a system, a structure, and a mindset of protection and abundance.

Family Two made a lot more money, but they didn't protect it, they didn't plan, and within two generations, all of it was gone, spent on immediate gratification, lifestyle upgrades, and here-and-now thinking. That's the danger of not having a legacy plan in place. It doesn't matter how much you make—it's how much you keep and how well you preserve it.

Why Families Lose Wealth (and Pass on Debt Instead)

So why do so many families fail at this? Why do they pass on debt—or worse, conflict—instead of wealth?

Honestly, it boils down to one word: influence.

All it takes is one person, just one family member with a strong personality and the wrong priorities, to derail everything. Maybe they didn't grow up with much and feel like they finally deserve the good life. Or perhaps they've always had it easy and think it'll just keep flowing no matter what. Either way, they make decisions based on entitlement, not responsibility.

That's why I believe so strongly in family governance. You need to have guardrails in place. You need to surround your legacy with people who share your mindset and are committed to preserving it rather than exploiting it. If you don't have that, you risk letting private agendas or short-term thinking ruin everything.

I've seen it happen too many times. Jealousy creeps in. People try to one-up each other. You get that "Keeping Up with the Joneses" mentality. And when the focus becomes "me, me, me" instead of "we," the foundation starts to crack.

If your family has never discussed legacy, if your predecessors didn't plan for this, then it's up to you to break the chain. That means having the courage to shift from pride and selfishness to purpose and stewardship.

Legacy Starts with Mindset and Family

Everything starts with mindset. You could hand someone a million-dollar business, a fully funded trust, or a real estate portfolio, but if their mindset is broken, it won't last. Everyone in your family must understand what abundance actually means and how to live it. Abundance is a lifestyle.

One of the most important shifts is moving from a consumer mindset to a producer mindset:

- Living below your means.
- Not needing to look wealthy.
- Thinking like an investor, not a spender.

- Building passive income so your money works for you while you sleep.
- Being methodical about how and where you spend your money so it comes back to you.

When your assets can pay for your lifestyle, and you've trained yourself to think long-term, you're living in abundance.

Family Matters

Legacy should be a group effort. Your estate team, financial professionals, and those carrying your legacy forward should be on the same page. My youngest brother and I discuss this a lot—we don't want it to stop with us. We want to create something that lasts. And I can tell you from experience that involving your family in this journey is essential.

Now, you have to be thoughtful. You can't bring in everyone just because they share your last name. As I mentioned earlier, sometimes people have private agendas, and giving the wrong person too much influence can throw everything off course. But the real magic happens when you bring in the right people who are like-minded and aligned with the bigger vision.

Family wealth, when handled with care and intention, can impact generations. It can provide freedom and opportunities that ripple outward for decades. Start the conversation. Maybe it's a casual outing or a retreat to begin talking about legacy, goals, and values. Keep it going with regular family meetings. Make space to discuss the big picture and how each person can contribute. Talk about what matters to you, what you want to support, and how you envision your wealth and wisdom helping others down the line.

Over time, you construct a family bank machine for abundance—a system of shared values, clear expectations, and collective purpose that is passed down, refined, and strengthened with every generation.

What We Don't Know
We're Passing Down

Most people don't even realize that money behavior is inherited. You don't just pass down your money. You pass down your habits. Your beliefs. Your patterns.

Many families pass down good habits, and when they do, they talk about them and teach them. But when bad habits are passed down, it's usually in silence. They happen without anyone saying a word and become the norm without being questioned. Some of the most common ones are:

- Collecting liabilities instead of assets.
- Prioritizing status symbols—cars, jewelry, phones, homes.
- Thinking that materialism equals success.
- Living above your means.
- Not budgeting, not planning for the future—short, mid, or long term.
- No emergency fund. No preparation for the unexpected.

- Even frugality is passed down as fear—always feeling like money is tight, even when it's not.

Sometimes, we inherit this chip-on-the-shoulder mentality that says, "I work hard, so I deserve this." Or worse, "This is just how our family is." But that doesn't have to be the end of the story. Your legacy can break those cycles. You can be the one who flips the script from scarcity to abundance, from surviving to thriving. And once that shift happens, everything changes.

How to Break the Cycle and Start Building Wealth—Even in Debt

Let's say you're not starting from abundance. You may be in debt, struggling to make ends meet, and this whole idea of legacy feels out of reach. But it's never too late to start. Even doing just a few of the right things consistently can shift everything in the right direction.

There are a ton of steps you can take, and you don't have to do them all at once. But if you pick even two or three and stick with them, you will build serious momentum.

1. Fund Your Emergency Cushion

Start small if you need to, but start. Every paycheck, set aside something—even just a few bucks—for unexpected expenses. Life will throw curveballs, and having that emergency fund in place keeps you from going into panic mode or racking up more debt when it happens.

2. Surround Yourself with the Right People

Jim Rohn said it best: "You are the average of the five people you spend the most time with." If you're the smartest or most successful person in your circle, it's time to find a new group. Join a mastermind. Attend meetups. Get around people who are doing better than you and inspire you to raise your game. You'll be surprised how much being in the right room can change your thinking and outcomes.

3. Prioritize Value Over Cost

When you look at your spending, stop asking, "How much does it cost?" Ask, "What value will this bring to my long-term life?" That one shift alone can transform how you approach everything, from the books you buy to the skills you invest in and how you manage your time.

4. Become a Lifelong Learner

This one's huge. Keep learning, keep reading, and keep growing. Whether you're sharpening an old skill or learning something completely new, the more knowledge and value you can bring to the table, the more valuable and marketable you become.

5. Shift to a Producer Mindset

Abundance comes when you stop just consuming and start producing. Ask yourself daily: "What can I create? What problems can I solve? How can I enrich someone else's life?" That's the path to sustainable wealth and impact.

6. Learn to Use Good Debt

Not all debt is bad. If you use debt strategically, borrowing at a low interest rate to invest in something that gives you a much higher return, that's a smart play. It's called arbitrage, and it's how wealthy people multiply their money. The key is ensuring your return far outweighs the cost of borrowing.

7. Nurture Valuable Relationships

Don't underestimate the power of people. Your network truly is your net worth. Get out there and talk to people. Attend events. Join communities. Ask how to bring value to someone else's life and be open to receiving the same in return. When you lean into the Law of Reciprocity, it has a way of opening doors you didn't even know existed.

From Rock Bottom to Abundant Legacy

You might be wondering, "Can people really turn it all around? Can someone go from nothing to building a legacy that lasts?" Absolutely.

I could share so many stories, but one that really stands out is Dr. Michael Duckett's journey. If you've never heard of him, I encourage you to look him up. His story is one of resilience, grit, and transformation that reminds you just how powerful your mindset and decisions can be.

Dr. Duckett was born into extreme poverty. In his early years, he was homeless, literally sleeping in abandoned buildings, just trying to survive. That kind of start doesn't usually scream "legacy builder." But he didn't let those circumstances define him. He used them.

He poured himself into education, self-discipline, and personal growth. He earned advanced degrees. He built multiple successful businesses. He became a speaker, an author, and a trainer—someone who didn't just pull himself out of hard times but who now uses that experience to lift others up.

His story reminds me a little of Tony Robbins, who also grew up in poverty and struggled in his early life. But like Tony, Dr. Duckett turned his past into fuel for something greater.

It's never about where you begin but what you do with it. Choose to rise and break cycles and shape the lives of everyone who comes after you. Wherever you're starting from, don't let that define your finish line. Let it inspire your legacy.

Be Intentional

Legacy is the stories, the wisdom, the values, and the hard-won lessons. It's the mindset, habits, and how you carry yourself through life. Yes, there will be some bad habits in the mix, as we all inherit a few things we wish we hadn't. But there will be good things, too. And those are the ones you want to shine a light on. Those are the ones you want to pass on. When your heirs, family, and even your community start implementing those principles in their personal and professional lives, you've done something that matters.

So don't just think in terms of wealth. Think in terms of abundance. Think about building something that's not here today and gone tomorrow but becomes part of who your family is.

KEY TAKEAWAYS

- ⮑ Building a true legacy involves passing down the mindset, habits, and values that created it in the first place.

- ⮑ Without intentional planning and family governance, even great wealth can disappear within two generations.

- ⮑ Your legacy should be a team effort with like-minded family members who share your long-term vision and are committed to preserving it.

- ⮑ You don't have to start from wealth to leave a legacy of abundance; even small, consistent actions taken today can spark massive change over time.

- ⮑ Breaking cycles of scarcity starts with shifting from a consumer mindset to a producer mindset and making decisions that serve your life and future generations.

CHAPTER EIGHT

SMART MONEY GOALS: YOUR MONEY WORKING FOR YOU

THE ULTIMATE GOAL—THE SMART MONEY GOAL—IS TO INVEST in something that pays. You have to think past something that covers your expenses and helps you survive to something that makes you money passively while you sleep. Instead of you working for your money, let your money work harder for you. You want the money you're saving to go into something that can double or triple over time. That mindset shifts you from being stuck in the daily grind to becoming someone focused on building wealth, creating freedom, and ultimately living on your terms.

Of course, there's trial and error. Not every opportunity is a good one. But there *are* elite products out there. It's just a matter of finding the right ones and then compounding your wins.

One of my colleagues, who is even younger than me, has a pretty impressive story. From his twenties, he had the mindset, mentorship, and focus on investing in income-producing assets right out of the gate. He wasn't born into wealth. He had a regular career. But because he made wise choices early, by the time he turned 40, he was done working for someone else. He was retired, just like that.

Now, he's built an enormous real estate portfolio, owns multiple businesses, and has his money working for him. He took advantage of things like cash value life insurance to fuel his investments, which became one of the big catalysts for everything else he was able to do.

He's in complete control of his time, his location, and his lifestyle. Money is just a byproduct because now he has time freedom, location freedom, and the freedom to be with family, travel, and live without being tethered to a job, boss, or clock.

Smart Investing

Smart investing puts you way ahead of the game. On day one, you're not going to start there. You probably don't have the baseline knowledge or experience yet, which is normal. However, the overarching goal should always be to begin investing in financial vehicles that give you excellent returns while giving you access to your money.

You don't want your money locked away where you can't touch it without penalties. Although you don't want your entire portfolio liquid, when you're ready to deploy capital on new, lucrative opportunities, you do. That's how you keep your money moving, how you keep it compounding, and how you create a well-oiled machine that just keeps growing.

A considerable part of thinking differently about money also comes down to one word: **taxes.** Taxes are a killer when it comes to your returns, whether it's capital gains, income taxes, or otherwise. If you don't plan for taxes strategically, you're giving away a huge chunk of your gains. When you set smart money goals, you must look at all the options available to you. Setting things up in a way that defers taxes or even eliminates them in some instances is a massive advantage. Then, once you build something you have control over, you can use the money you've made to go into even bigger deals.

Traditional savings methods seem safe on the surface, but they don't have the same upside. If everyone were using them, and it was the secret to real wealth, wouldn't everyone be wealthy? I always say, *"If you follow the herd, you will get herd results."*

Start thinking like the 1% or 2% who are truly ahead. Look at taxes, penalties, liquidity, cap amounts, control, and ownership. Those details separate traditional savings from the abundant, smart money mindset.

Build Systems That Save You Time, Energy, and Money

From day one, focus on building systems and automation that will make your money work for you. The sooner you put systems in place, the sooner you stop trading your time for money. I've seen a lot of people achieve serious success by implementing systems that create multiple streams of passive income. Here are just a few of the effective moves I've seen and used myself:

- **Real estate investing**, whether in residential or commercial real estate, can be a great way to generate passive cash flow once you have your properties up and running.

- **E-commerce stores:** Selling products online on autopilot without needing to be there every minute of the day.

- **Cash value life insurance:** The Abundant Wallet Method. It's liquid, defers taxes, and lets you use that capital to invest in real estate, fund businesses, or even run a private lending business.

- **Buying or creating businesses,** especially ones where you can hire others to run your operations, like franchises.

- **High-yield savings accounts:** If you've got a big lump sum, you can earn higher interest rates month after month without lifting a finger.

- **Annuities:** Particularly as you get closer to retirement age, these can give you predictable income for life.

- **Digital products:** Online courses, books, and eBooks. You create them once, and they keep generating income.

Many of these ideas are "set it up once, reap the rewards over and over" types of opportunities. That's the thinking you want to lean into.

And here's something I always remember:

SYSTEM stands for **Save YourSelf Time, Energy, and Money.**

If you keep that mindset, you'll naturally start looking for ways to automate, delegate, and optimize your financial moves.

Set SMART Goals

There are many different strategies for goal setting. One of the most common ones, and one that really works, is setting **SMART goals.** That's Specific, Measurable, Achievable, Relevant, and Timely. If you don't follow that pattern when setting your goals, something will fall short.

At the same time, I see people make another big mistake: they set goals that are way too aggressive or unrealistic. And when they don't hit them exactly on time, they get discouraged. Just because you don't hit a goal exactly on schedule doesn't mean you've failed. You may need an extra month or two. It's still a win.

Another goal-setting method I like is **PACT**—Purposeful, Actionable, Continuous, and Trackable. You've got to cut yourself some slack, especially when you're trying something for the first time. Remember that the real goal is progress, not perfection.

One quote I love and that I think about often comes from James Clear's *Atomic Habits*:

> **"If you get 1% better each day for one year, you'll end up 37 times better by the time you're done."**

You don't have to make giant leaps every day. You just have to do something today that you didn't do yesterday. I've seen many people change their lives by committing to small, consistent goals. Take a couple of financial advisors I know. They didn't start fast. They started slowly, doing the right things repeatedly, measuring their inputs and outputs, and staying consistent. They stuck to the plan. And now they're making $100,000 to $150,000 a month. That used to be a good *annual* salary. Now, it's their *monthly* income. That blows my mind.

I also have some real estate investing mentors who run a coaching and training business. They've been at it for over twenty years. It didn't happen overnight, but now they're making $250,000 a month. It's the product of staying committed, even when the road gets tough.

These are people who poured their blood, sweat, and tears into building something meaningful. And yes, they made mistakes early on, but they corrected them, adjusted, and kept moving. With the right mentors, strategies, and mindset, they turned their businesses into seven and eight-figure empires.

Write It Down

One simple trick that helped me a lot: years ago, I made a five-year plan and stuck it on my fridge. It wasn't fancy or complicated—I committed to doubling my real estate properties yearly.

The goal for year one? Buy one property. I ended up getting two.

In 2022, I planned for two more. I got four.

In 2023, I got four more.

In 2024, eight.

And now, in 2025, the goal is sixteen.

We've sold a few since then, and we've already got two or three new ones in the pipeline for the first half of the year. But what matters most is that *this system kept me moving.* That piece of paper I see daily reminds me how powerful goal-setting can be.

If you're setting goals because someone told you to or because it sounds good, you're just going through the motions. That's not enough. You have to *believe* you're going to achieve them. You have to *feel* it.

And one more thing that's imperative: **measurability.**

You have to track and measure your goals. What doesn't get measured gets missed. If you're off-track, you need to know how far off you are and what you need to tweak or pivot. It's the only way to keep your goals within reach and to actually hit them.

Tracking Progress Without Burning Out

Building wealth takes time. It takes experience. It takes patience. You have to start slow and steady to construct a real baseline. After that, compare your progress month after month, not to somebody else, but to yourself. I see so many people, myself included, fall into the trap of imposter syndrome. You look around and compare your level 2 to somebody else's level 10. That's not even a fair fight. I always tell my kids and remind myself: **Don't compare yourself to others. Compare yourself to your past self.** See where you were. See where you are now. See where you're going.

When you look at it that way, tracking your progress becomes a fun game—it's motivating. One of the best ways to do this is by measuring and analyzing your KPIs (Key Performance Indicators). Use software and systems to track how you're doing compared to where you started. You'll be astonished at how much you improve when you consistently measure the right things.

And it's important to celebrate those small wins. They matter. They build momentum.

You can also use productivity software to forecast where you're headed. Now, forecasting isn't a perfect science. But comparing your real numbers (your actuals) against your forecasts keeps you in tune with reality. It lets you pivot quickly when things don't go as planned. You can set up system alerts to let the technology tell you when something's off so you can catch it early, without stressing yourself out. And when challenges pop up, and they will, don't panic. Instead, create documented processes ahead of time for how you'll respond. That way, you're equipped with a strategic plan, not running around putting out fires.

There's no such thing as perfection. We're all works in progress. To tackle big goals, it takes a team and an open mindset to share ideas, brainstorm solutions, and learn along the way.

How to Balance Short-Term Fun with Long-Term Goals

Though it's a balancing act, you should be able to have fun *and* achieve long-term goals. I keep a few things in mind to make this happen.

First, living below your means is the foundation. It frees you up to take the vacations you want while you continue putting money into your retirement and investment planning. You're not sacrificing your future for a few good weeks today.

Personally, I like to plan out my vacations a year in advance. You know exactly when and how you'll take time off, and you save toward it little by little. Between those vacations, it's back to grinding, working hard, and staying committed to the long-term vision.

You need downtime and fun. If you don't, you're heading straight for burnout. So, it's just as important to plan for some short-term rewards as it is to keep your eye on the bigger goals.

When it comes to how I handle money, any distributions I make typically go right back into new investments that can grow even bigger over time. I'm in it for the long game. I know many people get a little short-sighted when they see a nice chunk of money because it's tempting to go out and spend big. But no matter how much or how little comes in, I always think about using it to set myself up even better for the future.

That said, I do carve out a portion specifically for vacations. I save for it months in advance and plan exactly how much I will spend so there are no surprises. I don't impulse buy. I'm super watchful. Most of the time, I return from vacation with money left over!

The key is to simultaneously have short-term, mid-term, and long-term plans in front of you. You're actively contributing to all of them—not just thinking about the big-picture dreams but drilling down into the steps it will take to get there.

And don't overthink it. Life happens. Sometimes you miss a goal. Sometimes you have to pivot. If something unexpected comes up, you may have to save a little longer or push that vacation back a few months. That's okay. The important thing is to stay flexible, detailed, and moving forward. The more thoughtful your planning is, the more likely your goals and results will come to life.

Start Small, Build Big: Your First Step Toward an Abundant Wallet

If you're ready to begin today, and I hope you are, I recommend establishing your savings foundation. Separate two savings accounts. One is your regular savings for short-term things—experiences, vacations, upgrades. The other should be a true emergency fund. I'm talking six months' worth of living expenses tucked away in a high-yield savings account where it can grow a little but, more importantly, be there when you need it.

Once you have that cushion, you'll breathe easier. You'll have some financial security, which can change how you think about money. Just make it a habit: anytime your savings or emergency fund dips down, make it a priority to refill it. Don't wait until you're scrambling in an emergency.

When you're ready to take the next step into investing, a great move to look into is house hacking. Buy a duplex or a triplex, live in one unit, and rent out the others. It's one of the most innovative ways to have your mortgage paid *for you* and create passive income at the same time. It's a real-world, doable strategy that can kickstart your journey toward financial independence.

You don't have to have it all figured out to start. You just have to start. Start with the savings habit. Start with one investment. Start with one system that helps your money work for you. Every small action you take today is a brick in the foundation of the abundant life you're building. And trust me—there's no better feeling than knowing you're moving closer, step by step, to complete freedom over your time, your money, and your future.

KEY TAKEAWAYS

- Focus on building wealth by investing in income-producing assets that give you time, location, and lifestyle freedom rather than just working for money.

- Prioritize liquidity, smart tax strategies, and financial vehicles that offer control and growth to keep your money moving and compounding over time.

- Create systems that automate income streams and make your money work for you, freeing up your time, energy, and mental bandwidth.

- Set SMART or PACT goals, track your progress consistently, and celebrate small wins without comparing yourself to others. Your only competition is your past self.

- Begin with a solid savings foundation, build toward smart investments like house hacking, and remember that small, consistent actions today lay the foundation for an abundant future.

EPILOGUE

"Like the air you breathe, abundance in
all things is available to you."
– Abraham Hicks

Congratulations on making it here. Most people never even think about taking control of their finances, let alone taking the steps you've taken. You showed up for yourself. And now, you have the tools, resources, and mindset to cultivate a truly abundant life filled with purpose, joy, and fulfillment.

By reading this book, you've equipped yourself with what I believe to be the most important step toward financial freedom: knowledge. You've learned how to shift your thinking, adopt new habits, and take control of your money instead of letting it control you. That transformation, going from overwhelmed or uncertain to confident and in command, is where abundance begins.

If you do nothing with this knowledge and go back to "business as usual," you'll miss out on a richer, more satisfying life. Staying stuck in your comfort zone may feel safe, but it comes at the cost of missed opportunities, untapped potential, and paths you never explored.

So what's next?

Let's open your mind to new possibilities and take this even further. Book a call with me and my team. Let's talk about what it truly takes to live financially free and abundantly without overcomplicating your life or working yourself into the ground.

Here's the simple 1-2-3 plan we'll walk through together:

1. **Discover your Wealth Roadmap**
2. **Implement your Asset Activation**
3. **Build Strategic Growth**

And once you have this plan in place, everything changes. You'll finally be able to take those vacations you've been dreaming about. You'll eliminate debt. You'll build a portfolio of assets that generate income while you sleep. You'll create freedom. You'll retire on your terms. And, most importantly, you'll leave a legacy that outlives you.

Ready to Unlock Your Financial Potential?

Schedule your free **Abundant Wealth Checkup** — a powerful session designed to help you grow, protect, and multiply your wealth. In just one conversation, you'll receive **17 key insights** that can help you:

- ✓ Build lasting financial security
- ✓ Identify hidden money leaks
- ✓ Use smarter strategies to accelerate wealth
- ✓ Align your money with your life goals

Take the first step to living a more abundant life — book your checkup today!

https://buildwithlarry.com/

ABOUT LARRY TUCH

Larry Tuch is a Data Engineer, Real Estate Investor, and Financial Strategist. Growing up in South Florida, Larry was happiest surrounded by family, soaking up the sun, and spending time with friends. His days were filled with hobbies like basketball, cooking, and traveling — and, like many kids, the occasional trouble.

As Larry got older, life's responsibilities took center stage. He became a proud father of two and built a successful career in the tech sector as a data engineer— a natural fit given his love for numbers. But over time, something changed. His work lost its appeal, becoming just a means to an end. Meanwhile, his financial life was slipping out of focus.

Despite enjoying many aspects of life, Larry struggled with debt and lacked a clear financial direction. That struggle eventually snowballed into $385,000 in debt. He felt overwhelmed, fearful, and defeated. Desperate for change, Larry began searching for answers.

In 2018, he made a pivotal decision. After separating from his ex-wife, he committed to understanding the psychology of money and what it truly takes to build wealth. Along the way, he uncovered deep-rooted fears about money formed in childhood, which had led to years of poor financial decisions. Earning, saving, investing — it all felt like a mystery.

Through years of trial and error, Larry became frustrated by the confusing and conflicting advice online. That's when the idea for *The Abundant Wallet* was born — a reliable source for people seeking clarity, guidance, and confidence around money.

Since then, Larry has transformed his life. He's now completely debt-free, owns ten real estate properties, has a healthy savings cushion, and is actively working toward a $10 million net worth. He's made a nearly $1 million swing, going from deeply in debt to holding over $550,000 in liquid assets and investments.

More importantly, Larry has mastered his money mindset, learned how to make intelligent financial decisions, and let his money work for him — not the other way around.

Today, *The Abundant Wallet* serves thousands of readers and followers looking to escape the cycle of debt, build wealth, plan for retirement, conquer financial fears, and gain the skills to take control of their financial futures. Larry's mission is simple: to help others create a life where money is not a constant worry but a powerful tool for freedom, security, and abundance.

"There's a particular kind of discomfort that comes from knowing you're capable of more—but not knowing where to start. That was me.

I had the ambition. The drive. Even the desire to do things differently—to live more intentionally, to build wealth on my terms, to create systems that actually served my life. But every time I sat down to "figure it out," I'd end up spinning in circles. I wasn't lacking ideas—I was lacking clarity. The question that kept me frozen was simple: What do I do first?

That question sounds small, but it can paralyze progress. I'd find myself staring at financial options, personal goals, big visions—and yet nothing moved. It was like standing in front of a whiteboard full of plans but with no marker in my hand. I felt stuck, not because I didn't believe in the future I wanted—but because I didn't know how to begin building it.

Then I met Larry.

Our first consultation wasn't flashy. It was honest. Grounded. He didn't try to impress me with jargon or sell me on a dream. Instead, he listened. Asked smart questions. Gave me options that actually made sense. More importantly, he helped me see what I hadn't been able to: that I wasn't as far off-track as I thought. I just *needed a guide. Someone to help me quiet the noise and build a plan of action—step by step, decision by decision.*

That's what Larry did. He gave language to the vague goals I had floating around in my head. He mapped out what to focus on now, what to put on the shelf for later, and how to move forward without burning out or second-guessing. Finally, I felt like the vision I had for abundance was actually possible. Not someday—soon.

Since that day, things have shifted. My mindset, for one. But also my actions. Conversations I used to avoid—I'm having. Moves I used to fear—I'm making. And the difference isn't just internal. I'm structuring my time and money differently. I'm asking smarter questions. I'm walking with a little more certainty.

If you're reading this wondering if working with Larry is worth it, let me say this: You don't need more hype. You need more clarity. That's what he gives you. He's not interested in quick wins or surface-level advice—he's here to help you build something sustainable. Something aligned. Something that makes sense for your life.

And the truth is, Larry and I connected because we're both wired the same way—we care deeply about leaving people better than we found them. We believe effort pays off. We believe in legacy, not just income. He's walked through his own transformation and now spends his time helping others do the same. That kind of leadership is rare. And I'm grateful our paths crossed."

- JoAnne Karagnara, Realtor, Strategist, Builder of Better Paths - Tampa, FL

"Before meeting Larry, my biggest challenge was understanding personal finances in a way that allowed me to make decisions today that would pay off in the future. I did not know the differences between the various types of insurance products or what would be the best fit for my family and our situation.

Honestly, it was embarrassing. I have an accounting degree and completed Financial Peace University, which would make you think perhaps I had a firm understanding of all things finance. This would be incorrect. I knew how to do a mean debt snowball but had no idea what to do once I was out of debt. I felt unprepared for the future in a way that I had no plan to address because I had no knowledge of the options available to me.

Prior to working with Larry, I only had a rough idea of my full financial picture. He encouraged me to create a spreadsheet with all my bills and income so that I could have a clear picture of where my money was going every month. I found multiple subscriptions that I didn't realize we were still paying for, and I was able to save $200 a month by canceling them. This in itself more than pays for the policy I purchased with Larry.

My husband has epilepsy and is not able to work. I now have peace of mind that if something happens to me, he will have enough money for my funeral expenses and to pay off our house so that he doesn't end up destitute. You can't put a price tag on that. I feel secure and grateful to have a clear understanding of where we are and where we're going.

Larry and his team organized multiple meetings with a variety of products based on what I was looking to accomplish. In addition to making sure I understood what I was purchasing and helping me get a full picture of my financial situation, they also made time for me after hours. We had multiple meetings after 5 pm, all over Zoom, which was very convenient. This was very important to me as I often work long hours and struggle to get things done during the day. They took the time to explain exactly what each plan would do carefully, and when I wasn't exactly satisfied with a particular solution, they put their thinking caps on and figured out a plan that better suited my needs. If you are looking for a financial planner who will listen to you and find the right solution for you — not just the easy answer — Larry and his team are the ones for you."

- Brianna Peterson., RP&G Printing - Lutz, FL

***

"Larry helps clients identify areas of financial need and implements a method to help them gain financial freedom. I did not have that chance until I was well into my adult life, so for anybody to have that opportunity to better their finances is extremely important.

Larry's clients have peace of mind. That's the number one thing I could say about Larry. Once he gets them through his process, they can live with peace of mind that their family will be taken care of and the legacy will go on. He has set up himself and several people close to him for a sustainable retirement.

If you're on the fence about working with Larry, get to know the guy because he's very genuine, wants to help take care of everything, and ensures you get what you want out of his services. I want to add that Larry believes in God, Jesus Christ, our Lord, and wants to be honorable and ethical when caring for his clients and those around him."

- Jason D. Murray, Entrepreneur: Financial Services, Martial Arts, and Personal Development - Oklahoma City, OK

www.ingramcontent.com/pod-product-compliance
Lightning Source LLC
Chambersburg PA
CBHW070933210326
41520CB00021B/6927